The wisdom of the brother of Jesus

Reading James Today

John Dickson

AQUILA
PRESS

A book by Aquila Press

James - The wisdom of the brother of Jesus
Published November 2006

Aquila Press, PO Box A287, Sydney South, Australia 1235
Ph: (612) 8268 3344
Fax: (612) 8268 3357
Email: sales@youthworks.net
www.publications.youthworks.net

NATIONAL LIBRARY OF AUSTRALIA
ISBN 1 921137 64 9
Cover Design by Joy Lankshear

Contents

Foreword

I welcome John Dickson's commentary on James to our growing 'library' of commentaries. John is multi-gifted, as evangelist, scholar, author and musician. He is, however, also an experienced pastor and he applies the practical teachings of James in a down to earth way. John Dickson's James, like other commentaries in this series, is based on high level scholarship, yet is expressed in straightforward language. It indicates that 'local talent' is of a very high order.

My prayer is that through John Dickson's explanations, the message of James will come alive to individuals and groups who read this wonderful letter.

Paul Barnett
Series Editor

1

The Significance of James

Introduction to the letter

The modern tendency to dissect, analyse and probe the words of Scripture can, if we are not careful, cause us to miss its intended force. This is no truer than with the epistle of James. James, more than most books in the Bible, shoots straight from the hip, as it were. He has little time for sophisticated rhetoric and fine argumentation; he wants simply and urgently to call on believers to look like real believers. His message is fast and (at times) furious but it is always sprinkled with grace. Whether it is his stinging rebuke of the world's bias toward the rich (2:1–13) or his evocative warning about the poisonous power of the tongue (3:1–12), James has a knack of highlighting common deviations from Christ's path of love and drawing readers back into a humble recognition of their need for divine mercy. Allowing ourselves to be 'found out', as it were, and then submitting ourselves to the gracious hand of God are the keys to reading (and commenting upon) this important portion of God's word.

But not everyone has felt warmly about the letter of James.

THE 'EPISTLE OF STRAW'

The famous sixteenth century Reformer, Martin Luther, the man at the foundation of the Protestant church, described the letter of James as *ein rechte stroern Epistel*, 'a right epistle of straw'. In the famous Luther Bible, published throughout Europe in 1522, Luther arranged to have James placed at the back of the volume without a page reference in the Table of Contents (though, in later editions, he thought better of this idea).

Why such a low view of a biblical book from the founder of the Protestant tradition? First, there is the apparent contradiction in the book between Paul's doctrine of salvation by grace through faith (Ephesians 2:8) and James' insistence:

> You see that a person is justified by what he does and not by faith alone. (James 2:24)

Since Paul's thought is more widely attested in the New Testament than is James', the epistle of James, thought Luther, had to take a back seat.

Secondly, and relatedly, the epistle of James contains no obvious reference to the death and resurrection of Jesus. This is odd, thought Luther, and illustrates the suspect nature of this ancient Christian writing.

Luther's concerns over James have been expressed in less extreme ways by many over the years. Compare the number of evangelical commentaries on this epistle with the number written on any one of the Apostle Paul's letters. I estimate the figure is about 1:3. The anxiety over James is completely ill-founded. When we arrive at James 2:14–26 I hope to show that, while Paul and James are saying different things to different audiences, their views on 'faith' and 'works' are consonant and not contradictory at all.

As for the lack of references in James to the death and resurrection of Jesus, two things must be remembered. Firstly, James' interests in this letter are more practical than theological. His work focuses on the details of Christian living rather than on the *basis* for Christian living. Immorality not heresy was the problem among James' first readers—or 'hearers' since, like many ancient letters, James was almost certainly designed to be read out loud to its recipients.

Secondly, while it is true that Jesus' death and resurrection are not taught in the letter, they are assumed—particularly the resurrection. In Chapter 2:1, for instance, James describes Jesus as 'our glorious Lord Jesus Christ' or literally 'our Lord Jesus Christ *of the glory*'. This expression only makes sense within the early Christian belief that Jesus has entered into resurrected glory at the right hand of God. Jesus himself described his resurrection (and ascension to God's right hand) as 'entering glory' (Luke 24:26). The Apostle Paul follows suit in Philippians 3:21 speaking of the risen Christ's 'body of the glory' (literal translation). The references in the letter to the return of Jesus (James 5:7–9) also assume Jesus' heavenly glory.

James does not provide a comprehensive theological account of our faith as Paul does in, say, Romans. Nor does he give us a riveting historical account of the faith as does Luke in the book of Acts. He does, however, offer one of the most compelling portraits of Christian living anywhere in the Bible. In this sense, James is anything but an 'epistle of straw'. And, as we shall see, there is a sense in which James has a deeper affinity with the traditions of Jesus than does any book of the Bible outside the four Gospels.

THE STYLE OF JAMES

Unlike most letters in the New Testament James contains not a linear argument combating some doctrinal misunderstanding but a rapid-fire set of direct and, for the most part, very clear 'aphorisms', or proverbial sayings, concerning the right way to act in God's world. Consider this selection of statements:

> Judgment without mercy will be shown to anyone who has not been merciful. (2:13)
>
> All kinds of animals, birds, reptiles and creatures of the sea are being tamed and have been tamed by man, but no man can tame the tongue. (3:7–8)
>
> Humble yourselves before the Lord, and he will lift you up. (4:10)
>
> Be patient, then, brothers, until the Lord's coming. See how the farmer waits for the land to yield its valuable crop and how patient he is for the autumn and spring rains. (5:7)

In just about every paragraph of the letter readers are challenged to modify their lives in conformity with God's will. There is little explanation or persuasion: there is just wave after wave of authoritative pronouncements about the life demanded of the follower of Jesus. The style no doubt sounds familiar. Consider these sayings of Jesus:

> Blessed are the merciful, for they will be shown mercy. (Matthew 5:7)
>
> Whoever has will be given more; whoever does not have, even what he has will be taken from him. (Mark 4:25)
>
> The good man brings good things out of the good stored up in his heart, and the evil man brings evil things out of the evil stored up in his heart. (Luke 6:45)
>
> ... everyone who exalts himself will be humbled, and he who humbles himself will be exalted. (Luke 18:14)

Jesus was the master of the rapid-fire, aphoristic style of preaching and James, more than any other New Testament writer, has inherited this style. Moreover, the letter of James contains more quotations and allusions to the sayings of Jesus than does any other book in the New Testament. To list but a few:

James 2:2–4 = Luke 20:46;
James 2:8 = Matthew 22:39–40;
James 2:13 = Matthew 5:7;
James 3:18 = Matthew 5:9;
James 4:9 = Luke 6:25;
James 5:2 = Matthew 6:19–20;
James 5:12 = Matthew 5:34–37.

I will draw attention to these and others throughout the commentary. The most obvious example is found in James 5:12:

> Above all, my brothers, do not swear—not by heaven or by earth or by anything else. Let your 'Yes' be yes, and your 'No', no, or you will be condemned.

Tellingly, James does not present these words as a quotation of Jesus, even though everyone in his audience must have heard the echo of Jesus words now found in Matthew 5:34–37:

> But I tell you, Do not swear at all: either by heaven, for it is God's throne; or by the earth, for it is his footstool; or by Jerusalem, for it is the city of the Great King. And do not swear by your head, for you cannot make even one hair white or black. Simply let your 'Yes' be 'Yes,' and your 'No', 'No'; anything beyond this comes from the evil one.

What James lacks in concrete references to the events of Jesus' death and resurrection he more than makes up for in his consistent reliance upon the style and content of Jesus' teaching.

WHICH JAMES?

There may be a very good explanation for James' strong affinity with the sayings of Jesus. The two were very likely brothers.

James introduces himself to us in the opening line of the epistle simply as "James, a servant of God and of the Lord Jesus Christ" (1:1). But to which James does this refer? There are three main Jameses mentioned in the New Testament: (1) the Apostle James, son of Alphaeus (Matthew 10:3); (2) another apostle James who was the son of Zebedee and brother of the apostle John (Matthew 10:2), and (3) James the brother of Jesus (Mark 6:3). The first James drops out of sight after his mention in the list of apostles (Matt 10:3; Acts 1:13). The second James, while appearing with his brother John (son of Zebedee) on several occasions in the Gospels, is mentioned only twice in the book of Acts, once in a list of apostles in Acts 1:13 and then again in Acts 12:2 where his martyrdom (circa AD 41/42) is reported in passing: "He (Herod) had James, the brother of John, put to death with the sword."

Our third James (the brother of Jesus) moves from relative obscurity in the Gospels (Matthew 13:55; Mark 6:3) to a place of great prominence in the Book of Acts. In Acts 12:17, 15:13 and 21:18 James appears as the central leader of the Jerusalem church, the 'mother church' of the burgeoning Christian movement. The letters of Paul confirm this central role of James the brother of Jesus (1 Cor 15:7; Gal 1:19; 2:9–12).

The prominence in early Christianity of this third James makes him the most natural candidate for the author of the epistle bearing this name, especially when we note that the letter is formally addressed to "the twelve tribes scattered among the nations", that is, to the Jewish-Christian communities throughout the Roman world. From what we know of first century Christianity only one 'James' possessed the kind of universal authority among Jewish believers that this formal introduction assumes: James, the brother of Jesus and head of the mother church.

The early church was unanimous about who wrote this epistle. The brother of the Lord was the only candidate ever proposed. Even those who thought the letter might be pseudonymous (i.e., written under a false name) knew that the 'James' referred to in the title was meant to be the son of Mary, the brother of Jesus.

What about modern scholarship? It must be said that numerous scholars over the years have doubted this epistle was written by the brother of Jesus. This is not because they propose that one of the other Jameses wrote the letter; it is because they regard the epistle as pseudonymous. Two reasons have been advanced for this conclusion: (1) the Greek of the epistle is too sophisticated to have been written by a Palestinian (Aramaic-speaking) peasant Jew such as James; (2) the letter was finally accepted by the early church as 'Scripture' only relatively late in the piece. This is difficult to explain, say some scholars, if the epistle had been penned by someone of James' prominence.

Both points are roundly refuted by a growing number of critical scholars. On the question of the Greek of the epistle, several things can be said. Firstly, although James was born and raised in Aramaic-speaking Galilee, he spent the last three decades of his life (AD 30–62) in the bustling international city of Jerusalem where many people (including many Jews) spoke Greek as their *first* language (Acts 9:29). Indeed, we know that from the beginning the Jerusalem church had a siseable community of Greek-speaking Jewish converts (Acts 6:1). It is not at all difficult to imagine the head of the Jerusalem church becoming proficient in the Greek language over the course of three decades. In any case, secondly, in an official letter such as this it is highly probable that the services of a Greek-speaking scribe (readily available in Jerusalem) were called upon to produce the finished, polished product. This was commonplace in antiquity. Even the Apostle Paul, who was fluent in Greek, used a scribal secretary, or amanuensis, from time to time (Rom 16:22). Thirdly, although the letter is written in able Greek, it is a Greek sprinkled with 'Semitisms', expressions of grammar and phraseology influenced by Aramaic forms of speaking. Scholars list the following Semitisms: James 1:6, 9, 11, 13, 21; 2:6; 3:6; 4:8– 9; 5:4, 7, 9, 11, 20). This indicates a Greek-speaking author with an Aramaic background. The head of the Jerusalem church fits this description easily.

But what about the early church's slow confirmation of the epistle of James as a part of the canon of Scripture: does this imply some doubt about the authorship? The answer is: not necessarily. It is true that the letter is cited infrequently by early Christian writers. However, this suggests only that the letter was not very popular in the mainstream Gentile churches of the second and third centuries. This fact is easily explained by the simple observation that Jewish Christianity had all but died out by this period. A letter explicitly addressed to *Jewish* believers (1:1) was unlikely to have held much interest for the now principally *Gentile* church, a point confirmed by the fact that, even when the letter was accepted as fully canonical, it continued to sit on the margins (as it still does for many today). In any case, the fact that Jewish Christianity was a fading memory by the second and third centuries virtually rules out the theory that someone in this period forged the epistle and tried to pass it off as a letter to Jewish Christians by the leader of Jewish Christianity. What purpose or audience would such a forgery serve?

Far more likely is the proposal, accepted by an increasing number of scholars, that this letter was in fact written by

James, the brother of Jesus, whose prominence in Christian history quickly faded but whose words are as powerful today as, I suspect, they were to those who first heard them.

THE LIFE OF JAMES

Let me step back, then, and offer a brief account of the life of James because I suspect, for some, the notion of Jesus having a brother at all, let alone one who grew up to be a leader in the church, might sound a little strange. Jesus in fact had four brothers and at least two sisters, and some are named in Mark 6:3:

> The people of Jesus' hometown said of him: "Isn't this Mary's son and the brother of James, Joseph, Judas and Simon? Aren't his sisters here with us?"

More striking than the mere existence of Jesus' nine-member family is the fact that during his public ministry, between AD 28–30, Jesus' family did not follow him. In a brief aside, the Gospel of John laments: 'For even his own brothers did not believe in him' (John 7:5). The Gospel of Mark reports this with brutal honesty: 'When Jesus' family heard about this, they went to take charge of him, for they said, "He is out of his mind"' (Mark 3:21). Not only did Jesus' family (presumably including James) not believe in him; they thought him insane. All the more striking, then, is the dramatic turn around we observe in Jesus' family in the days after his death. By May AD 30, just a few weeks after the crucifixion, Jesus' mother and brothers are in Jerusalem worshiping as a group with the other Christians:

> They [the apostles] all joined together constantly in prayer, along with the women and Mary the mother of Jesus, and with his brothers (Acts 1:14).

What happened between the public ministry of Jesus and May AD 30? According to the earliest piece of testimony about the resurrection, James saw something he could not deny:

> For what I received I passed on to you as of first importance: that Christ died for our sins according to the Scriptures, that he was buried, that he was raised on the

> third day according to the Scriptures, and that he appeared to Peter, and then to the Twelve. After that, he appeared to more than five hundred of the brothers at the same time, most of whom are still living, though some have fallen asleep. Then he appeared to James (1 Corinthians 15:3–7).

Having seen his resurrected brother with his own eyes James was a changed man. The one whom James had previously judged to be 'out of his mind' was henceforth revered as his Lord. How telling, then, is the introduction to the epistle: 'James, a servant of God and of the Lord Jesus Christ' (1:1)!

Jesus' other brothers (Joseph, Judas and Simon) may also have seen the risen Lord, or else they believed through James' testimony, for the next we hear of them they are travelling Christian missionaries: 'Don't we have the right' asks the Apostle Paul, 'to take a believing wife along with us, as do the other apostles *and the Lord's brothers* and Cephas?' (1 Cor 9:5). James, on the other hand, stayed in Jerusalem and over the next three decades rose to a prominence in the church that is rarely noted in popular Christian circles today. He presided over a church in Jerusalem of many thousands (Acts 2:41; 4:4).

If you were to ask mid-first-century Christians from anywhere in the Roman empire, 'Who was the earthly figure-head of the church?' they would almost certainly have said: 'James, the brother of the Lord.' Even Paul in Acts 21:18–25 defers to the authority of James. And in Galatians 2:9 he lists the 'pillars of the church' as James, Peter and John. The order is not accidental.

It is this great authority in the early church that gave James, and probably only James, the authority to pen a letter addressed 'to the twelve tribes scattered among the nations' (1:1), that is, to the many Christians of Jewish tribal descent living throughout the Empire. This letter, then, was a circular sent out from Jerusalem, the centre of ancient Christianity, by James, the pillar of ancient Christianity.

The significance of James in the first century is underlined by the fact that he rates a mention in a non-Christian work from the period. Flavius Josephus, the

Jewish military general, historian and aristocrat, writing toward the end of the first century tells us something about James that post-dates the events recorded in the New Testament. James was martyred for his faith in his brother.

> The younger Ananus, who had been appointed to the high priesthood, was rash in his temper and unusually daring. Possessed of such a character, Ananus thought that he had a favourable opportunity because Festus (Roman Governor) was dead and Albinus (new Roman Governor) was still on the way (AD 62). And so he convened the judges of the Sanhedrin and brought before them the one named James, the brother of Jesus who was called the Messiah, and certain others. He accused them of having transgressed the Jewish law and delivered them up to be stoned to death. (*Jewish Antiquities* 20.199–200).

From cynic and unbeliever to Christian leader and martyr: this was the life of James, the brother of the Lord.

Exactly *when* James wrote the letter we have before us is unknown. Theoretically, it could have been composed anytime between AD 48, when he appears to have risen to great prominence in the Jerusalem church (Acts 15:13–21), and his death in AD 62. Somewhere in the latter half of this timeframe is more likely.

We turn now to study James' words in all their striking, Christ-like authority.

2

The Brother of the Lord and the Tribes of Israel

James 1:1

> James, a servant of God and of the Lord Jesus Christ,
> To the twelve tribes scattered among the nations:
> Greetings (1:1).

The prescript, as it is called, is brief but full of interesting information. We have already explored the identity of this 'James': he is one of Jesus' four brothers and the leading 'pillar' of earliest Christianity. The name 'James' itself is an anglicised form of the Greek *Iakōbos* which, in turn, transcribes the Hebrew *Yaqob*, i.e. Jacob. The name was very important in biblical history, being first given to one of the great patriarchs of the Book of Genesis. Jacob (Gen 25:26) was grandson to Abraham, son to Isaac and father to twelve sons who would become the twelve tribes of Israel. James/ Jacob was henceforth a very popular name in Jewish history. As the figure head of the new 'twelve tribes of Israel' the brother of Jesus was very appropriately named.

All the more fascinating is the way James describes himself in relation to God and Jesus. He is a 'servant of God and of the Lord Jesus Christ'. The word 'servant' (Greek: *doulos* = 'slave') was frequently used in antiquity both as a title of humility and as a badge of honour. Trusted slaves in the emperor's household, for instance, were people of considerable importance. James here casts himself in just such a role—of humility and honour—in the service of God and, interestingly, of Jesus the Lord, the true emperor of the world. What follows in this letter, then, is an official pronouncement of one appointed as an imperial representative in the kingdom of God. The Apostle Paul also used the title *doulos*, slave/servant, to describe his commission in God's empire (Rom 1:1; Gal 1:10; Phil 1:1) as did Peter (2 Pet 1:1) and James' brother Jude (Jude 1).

It should be also noted that in describing himself as a slave of God *and Jesus*, in the same breath, James has elevated his brother to supreme authority. God the Father and the Messiah share mastery of his life. While it is probably going too far to suggest a reference here to Jesus' full divinity, it is probable James has in mind the early and widespread Christian affirmation that the Messiah has been exalted to God's right hand (Mark 14:62; Acts 2:33; Rom 8:34; Heb 1:3).

The official tone of the prescript carries over into the second half of verse 1: 'To the twelve tribes scattered among the nations: Greetings.' These words indicate that James' letter is a circular, a document designed for wide reading (and copying) throughout the Jewish Diaspora ('dispersion'). Ever since the period of the Great Exile (597–586 BC) large numbers of Jews could be found all over the pagan world. Significant Jewish communities had emerged in Babylonia, Persia, Egypt, Syria, Asia Minor, Greece and Italy. By the first century there were more Jews living in the Diaspora (between 5–8 million) than in the Holy Land itself (no more than 2 million).

How many of these Diaspora Jews ended up becoming Christians is anyone's guess. We do know that representatives from this vast Diaspora heard the gospel from the lips of Peter on the Day of Pentecost, just over a month after Jesus' resurrection:

> [5] Now there were staying in Jerusalem God-fearing Jews from every nation under heaven. [6] When they heard this sound, a crowd came together in bewilderment, because each one heard them speaking in his own language. [7] Utterly amazed, they asked: "Are not all these men who

> are speaking Galileans? [8] Then how is it that each of us hears them in his own native language? [9] Parthians, Medes and Elamites; residents of Mesopotamia, Judea and Cappadocia, Pontus and Asia, [10] Phrygia and Pamphylia, Egypt and the parts of Libya near Cyrene; visitors from Rome [11] (both Jews and converts to Judaism); Cretans and Arabs—we hear them declaring the wonders of God in our own tongues!" [12] Amazed and perplexed, they asked one another, "What does this mean?"
>
> [13] Some, however, made fun of them and said, "They have had too much wine."
>
> [14] Then Peter stood up with the Eleven, raised his voice and addressed the crowd: "Fellow Jews and all of you who live in Jerusalem, let me explain this to you; listen carefully to what I say" (Acts 2:5–14).

At the end of Peter's message that day we are told: 'Those who accepted his message were baptised, and about three thousand were added to their number that day' (Acts 2:41). Among these must have been Diaspora Jews who, returning to their lands, would have formed the beginnings of the communities to which James would later write.

In any case, James' intended readers (or hearers) are clearly Diaspora Jews who were 'believers in Jesus Christ' (2:1). They were Christian Jews. It is interesting, however, that nothing in the prescript indicates their *Christian* status. James refers to them simply as the 'twelve tribes', an Old Testament expression for the full complement of God's (Jewish) people. The point is significant historically and theologically.

Historically, it is important to remember that the first Christians (of Jewish descent) did not see themselves as 'Christians'. They were simply members of Israel for whom the Messiah had come. It was not until the end of the first century and the beginning of the second that Jewish believers in Jesus (what we call Christians) were formally and widely rejected by their wider Jewish family. Theologically, it is important to note that what we call Christianity is the fulfilment and not rejection of the hopes of biblical Israel. The phrase 'twelve tribes' as a designation of (Jewish) Christian believers underlines this point well.

This is not to say that the epistle of James is only relevant to Christians of Jewish descent. Far from it. The teaching of this letter provides wonderful evidence of how the first (Jewish) Christians completely transformed what it meant to obey the God of Israel. At the centre of new covenant life is not the law of Moses (the Torah) but the wisdom of the Messiah Jesus. This will become evident as we continue through the letter. It is the explicit teaching of Christ that forms the new law of the new Israel.

REFLECTIONS

1. The authority of the epistle. The voice of James is an authoritative one. The prescript reminds us that as we read the epistle we are listening not merely to the personal reflections of a member of Jesus' family but the divinely sanctioned words of an imperial 'slave' in God's kingdom. In the ancient world, to reject an official message delivered by an imperial slave was to reject the emperor himself—slaves were often *representatives* as much as servants. Likewise, the prescript casts a strong note of authority over the entire epistle. To reject the message that follows—however great its demands—is to reject God and Christ themselves.

Martin Luther should have known better than to relegate James simply because his interpretation of the book didn't fit with his theological viewpoint. We too, all these years later, should know better than to stand in judgment of James' words, no Matthewer how much they challenge our lifestyle or 'theology'. For through these words the glorious risen Messiah, seated at God's right hand, continues to mediate his message to the church.

2. Our Old Testament roots. We are also reminded in the prescript of the essentially Jewish nature of Christian faith. The reference to the 'twelve tribes' and the absence of any 'Christian' indicator in verse 1 underlines the continuity, in the mind of James and his readers, between faith in Jesus and the promises given to Israel.

In different periods of church history the Old Testament context of Christian faith has been overlooked and sometimes rejected altogether. In the second century, for instance, an influential Christian leader named Marcion set about to produce a New Testament completely devoid of Old Testament dependence. Of course, Marcion was rejected as a heretic, but the tendency to ignore the Jewish, or Old Testament, background to our faith lingers on in more subtle forms. But we neglect the covenantal (Old Testament) context of our faith to our peril. Unless we appreciate how it is that Jesus fulfills the hopes of the 'twelve tribes of Israel' our faith will be less than truly Christian.

3. *The miracle of James' conversion.* The transformation of James the brother of Jesus should be a cause for Christian rejoicing. A doubter and unbeliever was captured by the majesty of the risen Lord so that he devoted the rest of his life to serving the One he previously denied. As we rightly give thanks for the miracle of the conversion of the Apostle Paul, so we rightly rejoice in the story of the Lord's own brother who, like Paul, gave his life for the testimony concerning God's Messiah. Such was the certainty of James' faith in the Lord Jesus Christ.

QUESTIONS FOR DISCUSSION

1. What is so significant about James' transition from being an 'unbeliever', to a devoted Christian, church leader and eventually martyr for Jesus?
2. What do you feel is the significance of James' description of himself as a 'servant (slave) of God and of the Lord Jesus Christ'? To what extent can this—should this—be said of every Christian?
3. Why is the first covenant, the Old Testament, so important to Christian faith? Think of some specific examples.

3

The Gift of Wisdom

James 1:2–18

While reading through James 1:2–27 it is striking that virtually every paragraph appears to introduce a new and largely unconnected theme. This is partly a function of James' Jesus-like, aphoristic style, mentioned earlier. It also arises from the fact that Chapter 1 serves as an extended introduction, or executive summary, of all that follows. If the letter of James as a whole is an anthology of Christian living, Chapter 1 functions as a kind of contents page. Each paragraph in this opening section contains in miniature themes which will be explored more fully throughout Chapters 2–5. We begin with the first half of the introduction (1:2–18) in which James outlines the benefits of divine 'wisdom'.

WISDOM IN TRIALS (1:2–9)

The first paragraph of the introduction (1:2–8) holds some of the keys for understanding both the situation of the first hearers and the message of James to them.

> Consider it pure joy, my brothers, whenever you face trials of many kinds, because you know that the testing of your faith develops perseverance (1:2–3).

We do not know the details of the trials referred to by James but the rest of the letter provides some clues. In Chapter 2, as James warns against showing favouritism to the wealthy, he asks three exasperated rhetorical questions:

> Is it not the rich who are exploiting you? Are they not the ones who are dragging you into court? Are they not the

> ones who are slandering the noble name of him to whom you belong? (2:6–7).

Financial, legal and religious troubles are hinted at here. Christian hardship in the ancient world often involved significant social pressure.

Whatever the finer details of the trials mentioned in 1:2, the important thing James wants to say to these troubled believers is that such hardships can be counted 'pure joy' (verse 2). How so? James says it is by seeing trials as an opportunity to develop 'perseverance' in the faith. And, according to verse 4, perseverance 'must finish its work so that you may be *mature* and *complete*.' The word 'mature' is the Greek term *teleios* meaning 'perfect'. The term reappears in James' discussion of the tongue where the NIV renders it 'perfect': 'If anyone is never at fault in what he says, he is a perfect man' (3:2). While the English term 'perfect' has connotations of scoring 10/10 or of being sinless, the Greek term in biblical usage has more to do with fulfilling a goal or reaching a desired end than it does the absence of any blemish. Hence, the three expressions at the end of verse 4 are probably to be read as a piece: so that you may be (i) *mature* and (ii) *complete*, (iii) *not lacking anything*. The point, then, is that the trials experienced by Christians can, and should, be viewed in a broader perspective, as part of the journey toward being made whole. And, if Christian wholeness is an outcome believers value, they will be able to consider trials, in all their sad reality, as 'pure joy'.

There is one precious piece of luggage required for the journey toward Christian wholeness—'wisdom':

> If any of you lacks wisdom, he should ask God, who gives generously to all without finding fault, and it will be given to him (1:5).

Wisdom may seem like a strange necessity for times of trial—until we recall what the Bible means by the term. In modern usage 'wisdom' often means something like 'intelligence' or 'insight'. It is thought of in intellectual terms. But 'wisdom' in the ancient world, and especially in the Bible, was a feature of human *behaviour* as much as thought. From the Old Testament book of Proverbs, through the preaching of Jesus and into the book of James, 'wisdom' is *knowing how to live God's way in God's world.* Since the world is a creation of one God and therefore reflects his character, ultimate knowledge (wisdom) is knowledge of that character and its application to life in the world. To know how to act in accordance with God's will in the many and varied circumstances of life is to be wise. Consider the opening statement of the book of Proverbs:

> The proverbs of Solomon son of David, king of Israel: [2] for attaining wisdom and discipline; for understanding words of insight; [3] for acquiring a disciplined and prudent life, doing what is right and just and fair; [4] for giving prudence to the simple, knowledge and discretion to the young—[5] let the wise listen and add to their learning, and let the discerning get guidance—[6] for understanding proverbs and parables, the sayings and riddles of the wise.
>
> [7] The fear of the LORD is the beginning of knowledge, but fools despise wisdom and discipline (Prov 1:1–7).

James makes the ethical orientation of wisdom clear himself when he comes to expound the theme in Chapter 3:

> But the wisdom that comes from heaven is first of all pure; then peace-loving, considerate, submissive, full of mercy and good fruit, impartial and sincere (3:17).

Here 'wisdom' and the path of godliness are virtually indistinguishable. Coming back to 1:5, then, our great need in the midst of trials is not so much a better understanding of the Bible, or a fresh outpouring of God's Spirit. What we need is 'wisdom', clarity about how to live God's way in God's world.

How does one attain 'wisdom'? You 'ask God', says James, 'who gives generously to all without finding fault' (1:5). Wisdom is a gift. This too originates in the book of Proverbs: 'For the Lord *gives* wisdom' (1:6). The phrase 'without finding fault' underscores that it is the Lord's delight to offer wisdom to those who ask sincerely. He does not begrudge us his gift even if we are undeserving of it.

No sooner has James offered these words of comfort about God's generous, unbegrudging gift of wisdom than he adds what appears a harsh qualification:

> 6 But when he asks [for wisdom], he must believe and not doubt, because he who doubts is like a wave of the sea, blown and tossed by the wind. 7 That man should not think he will receive anything from the Lord; 8 he is a double-minded man, unstable in all he does (1:6–8).

The Lord's unreserved generosity toward his children does not extend to doubters. What does James mean by this? The English words 'believe' and 'doubt' are mainly cognitive terms. To 'believe' often means little more than to assent to the truth of something; to 'doubt' means to question the truth of something. In biblical usage, however, the words 'believe' and 'doubt' refer not to the presence and absence of mere 'assent' but to the presence and absence of *trust* or *devotion*. To believe in God, or to have 'faith' in him ('belief' and 'faith' are the same word in Greek: *pistis*), is not merely to *acknowledge* God's existence; it is to *entrust* oneself to him. To 'doubt' God is to *refuse to entrust* oneself to him. James is not saying one must be confident of the outcome of the request before God will grant it. Verse 6 reads literally: 'Let him ask *in faith*, not doubting.' The point is, when one asks God for wisdom—for knowledge of his ways in this world—one must do so in an attitude of sincere devotion to the Lord.

Those taking an each-way-bet, on the other hand, those who have entrusted themselves partly to God and partly to the world, should not expect to receive anything from the Lord. Such a person, says James in verse 8, is 'double-minded', literally 'split-souled' (*di-psychos*). In colloquial English we might say 'two-faced'. The word underlines the point of verse 6: James is not speaking against 'doubt' in the cognitive sense of the term; he is reminding his readers that God is no fool. To receive God's gifts one must not be a hypocrite, feigning Christian commitment while secretly devoting oneself to the ways of the world.

As we continue through the epistle it will become clear that double-mindedness is precisely the problem for some in James' audience. While the first readers were enduring hardships at the hands of those above them, ironically, many of them were also treading down those beneath them. They were 'insulting the poor' (2:6) and clambering over one another in an effort to climb the social ladder (4:2– 3). Indeed, the central paragraph of the letter (4:7–10) will call for repentance from these split loyalties: 'Wash your hands, you sinners, and purify your hearts, you double-minded' (4:8). These, then, are the people who should not expect to receive anything from the Lord—unless, of course they repent.

This first paragraph of James' executive summary of the letter provides, as noted earlier, some of the keys to the whole epistle. Central here is the place of wisdom. Knowing how to live God's way in God's world (through the trials and joys of life) is the principal means of attaining spiritual steadfastness and completion. It is a divine gift to be sought with single-minded devotion to the Lord.

PRIDE AND HUMILITY, RICHES AND POVERTY (1:9–11)

The next few verses strike another recurring theme of the letter: godly economics.

> [9] The brother in humble circumstances ought to take pride in his high position. [10] But the one who is rich should take pride in his low position, because he will pass away like a wild flower. [11] For the sun rises with scorching heat and withers the plant; its blossom falls and its beauty is destroyed. In the same way, the rich man will fade away even while he goes about his business (1:9–11).

The ideas hinted at in this paragraph will emerge with force in 2:1–13 (a warning against favouring the rich), 2:14–19 (a call for works of mercy to the poor), 4:1–6 (a rebuke to those who crave financial gain) and 5:1–6 (a pronouncement of judgment upon wealthy oppressors). Here in Chapter 1, James preempts the theme calling on believers, regardless of their station in life, to view their situation theologically not socially. The 'humble' believer is the one who is economically poor. He should 'take pride', says James, in his 'high position'. The contrast here between 'humble' and 'high' is neat since the word translated 'humble' comes from the Greek word 'low'. The high position the poor believer is to ponder is, of course, that of being a follower of the true Lord of the world. To be a Roman citisen was a great honour in the ancient world. To be a citisen of the kingdom of Christ is an even greater prise. The poor Christian can take pride in this knowledge confident that one day God will lift up the lowly and bring down the high and mighty (4:6–10; 5:1–6). The phrase 'take pride' means more than simply to feel good about oneself. It means *to exult*, to be jubilant in some victory or achievement. God's acceptance of the poor believer, and promise one day to exalt him or her, is a cause of true jubilation.

The rich Christian, on the other hand (1:10), is to contemplate his or her *low* (Greek: 'humble') position. Even the wealthy will pass away. The rich of this world are not lords over creation (despite their aspirations to be so); they are simply creatures within it, akin to the 'wild flower' which is scorched by the Middle Eastern sun and withers away. Just as the poor are to think of themselves in light of their glorious redemption in Christ, so the rich are to remind themselves of their passing nature as fleeting parts of the creation. James will have much more to say about these themes as the letter unfolds.

LIVING FOR A FUTURE CROWN (1:12)

One aspect of true wisdom—of clarity about God's ways—is an understanding of the endpoint of our existence. In 1:12 James stresses that the Christian life is to be lived in light of the future:

> Blessed is the man who perseveres under trial, because when he has stood the test, he will receive the crown of life that God has promised to those who love him (1:12).

At one level, these words continue the theme of 'trials' from 1:2. At another, they flag the theme of judgment and reward which pervades much of the rest of the letter (2:13; 3:1; 5:3–9). The sentence is a 'beatitude', a statement of divine blessing, and reminds us of Jesus' famous Beatitudes in Matthew 5:3–10. The last of Jesus' Beatitudes has significant resonance with the words of James:

> Blessed are those who are persecuted because of righteousness, for theirs is the kingdom of heaven (Matthew 5:10).

If the 'trials' James mentions here include being slandered for Jesus' name, as James 2:7 indicates, the ideas expressed in these two beatitudes are quite close.

The particular blessing mentioned by James is the 'crown of life', a metaphor taken from the sporting arena of the ancient world. As the Apostle Paul says:

> Everyone who competes in the games goes into strict training. They do it to get a crown that will not last; but we do it to get a crown that will last forever (1 Cor 9:25).

Several New Testament authors employ the image of a future 'crown' (1 Thess 2:19; 2 Tim 4:8; 1 Pet 5:4). Revelation 2:10 uses exactly the same phrase: 'Be faithful, even to the point of death, and I will give you the *crown of life.*'

The crown to which James refers is 'life' itself, a place in God's eternal kingdom. This 'life', says James, is guaranteed by the promise of God to those who love him, to those who fulfill the greatest commandment (Deut 6:5; Matthew 22:37- 38). It is not 'good people' as such who receive this life; it is those who are in a right relationship with God and who love him. James will have a lot more to say about living in light of the future judgment.

SIN AND DEATH (1:13–15)

The Greek word *peirasmos* can mean either 'trial' in the sense of *hardship* or 'temptation' in the sense of *attraction toward sin.* Having used the word in the first sense in verse 2 and verse 12, James moves seamlessly in the next paragraph to employ the term in the other sense. The two ideas are not separate of course. Often hardship in one's faith raises fresh temptations to abandon our love of God:

> [13] When tempted, no-one should say, "God is tempting me." For God cannot be tempted by evil, nor does he tempt anyone; [14] but each one is tempted when, by his own evil desire, he is dragged away and enticed. [15] Then, after desire has conceived, it gives birth to sin; and sin, when it is full-grown, gives birth to death (James 1:13–15).

Again, the collection of ideas raised here (temptation-sin-death) will become a major focus of the teaching of the letter. In 3:1–12 James will talk about the struggle to restrain the deadly power of the tongue. In 4:1–10 he will warn his hearers not to be enticed by a desire for wealth and pleasure which brings the judgment of God, the ultimate death.

James wants his readers to know that the path from temptation to sin then to death is not an inevitable one; it is not fixed by the will of God as if he were doing the tempting (1:13). It is rather the result of our own 'desire'—the NIV adds 'evil' but it is not in the Greek text. When we allow desire to conceive, that is, to fix upon some evil intention, then sin is born. And sin, says James, when it grows to maturity, will be the death of us. James' point is that instead of blaming God for our temptations we must keep our desires in check before they conceive. Desire and temptation are not in themselves sin; but they certainly lead there if they are not dealt with firmly. Much of the remainder of the letter is a plea to resist such desires and temptations.

GOD'S GIFTS FROM ABOVE (1:16–18)

Having mentioned the temptations from *within*, James now turns to the gifts from *above*:

> [16] Don't be deceived, my dear brothers. [17] Every good and perfect gift is from above, coming down from the Father of the heavenly lights, who does not change like shifting

> shadows. [18] He chose to give us birth through the word of truth, that we might be a kind of firstfruits of all he created (1:16–18).

The theme of being 'deceived' (*planaō*, literally 'led astray') emerges again in the concluding paragraph of the epistle: 'My brothers, if one of you should *wander* (*planaō*) from the truth' (5:19). That some in his readership might be led astray from God's truth appears to be a key concern of James. Many potential deviations from God's path are treated in the letter (2:17–20; 3:14–15; 4:13–17)—all of them ethical rather than doctrinal.

Far from sending 'temptations', God in fact sends good and perfect gifts (verse 17). These come down 'from above', from the Father of the 'heavenly lights', a reference to God's creation of the heavenly bodies (Gen 1:14–19). But what are these gifts of the Father?

They are twofold.

Part of the answer is found in the following verse: 'He chose to give us birth through the word of truth' (verse 18). Having mentioned the 'birth' of sin-and-death in the previous paragraph, James here urges us to contemplate afresh the greater birth, the one which came about through our hearing and trusting God's true word, the message of Jesus (the precise content of this 'word' will be discussed in my comments on 1:22).

This point deserves emphasis. According to James, our spiritual birth as children of God is a gift from above not a payment for work carried out here below. No Matthewer how strident James' insistence on good works appears in this epistle, his starting point is here: our spiritual birth is a gift. It comes, furthermore, from the hands of One who 'does not change like shifting shadows' (verse 17). Our salvation, therefore, is premised not on our incomplete efforts at obedience but on the immovable character of God.

The 'gifts from above' almost certainly also include the gift of 'wisdom' as well. James has already described wisdom as a divine gift given to all who ask (1:5). Moreover, when James again speaks of that which comes 'from above', it is a reference to the heavenly gift of wisdom. In 3:15–17 he contrasts wisdom which 'does not *come down from heaven*' (literally: 'come down from above') with 'the wisdom that *comes from heaven*' (literally: 'from above'). The connection with 1:17 is clear.

In saying that the gifts from above (1:17–18) include both 'birth through the word of truth' and 'wisdom' I do not wish to imply that these things are separate. In James' mind they are two sides of the one coin. The word of truth is simply the message of Jesus. Believing that word brings new birth and applying that word to daily life is what wisdom is all about. One need only read the Gospels to realise that accepting Jesus entails accepting the path of wisdom he preached.

In the second half of verse 18 James moves seamlessly from a birth metaphor to an agricultural metaphor. The purpose of our new birth by the word of truth is 'that we might be a kind of firstfruits of all he created'. The expression 'firstfruits' is straight out of the Old Testament where it describes the initial portion of a crop (before the full harvest) which was to be set apart for God (Exodus 23:16–19; Numbers 18:13). Two ideas, then, are perhaps present in James' description of believers as 'firstfruits': Christians are set apart for the Lord and they are a sign of the coming harvest when God grants new birth to all of creation. Paul uses the image of 'firstfruits' to refer (i) to Christ's resurrection (1 Cor 15:20– 23), the sign and guarantee of our own resurrection, and (ii) to the gift of the Holy Spirit (Rom 8:23), the foretaste of the reign of the Spirit in the age to come. The 'firstfruits' expression highlights that just beneath this highly ethical and practical epistle lies a robust eschatology. It is no exaggeration to say that the entire letter is a call to live now in light of the age to come.

REFLECTIONS

1. Ethics over intelligence. The ethical orientation of true understanding, of wisdom, stands in marked contrast to the values of contemporary society. Our world prises knowledge, intelligence and shrewdness while often ignoring the need for virtue. 'Wisdom' has been emptied of its foundational and biblical content. Christians, however, are called to value godliness over cleverness, compassion over knowledge, generosity over financial advancement and justice over intellectual achievement. To do so is to be truly wise.

2. Living for the future. James' perspective on trials poses a challenge to society's emphasis on the importance of living for now. Living for the moment is completely counter-intuitive to the perspective of James (and Jesus). The reign of God has begun, the Messiah's glory has been established (1:1; 2:1): believers are now to wait and live as those who know the future, who know that evil will be overthrown (5:1–6) and that the Messiah will return to establish righteousness (5:7–11). Christian living is anticipatory living, conforming now to the unseen kingdom which is to come.

3. *God's provisions.* As challenging as James' call for godly perseverance appears, his words are not without encouragement to the believer to rest in the marvellous provisions of God. Inadequacies in the Christian life should not cause despondency; they should motivate us to pray for a deeper experience of God's gifts (of wisdom). Moreover, we must recall that our position before God derives not from our intentions and resources but from his choice, his gift and his word.

QUESTIONS FOR DISCUSSION

1. The three most important words in James 1:2–4 are joy, perseverance and maturity. In your own words, what is the logical connection between these ideas?

2. Is there any contradiction between the statement that God 'gives generously to all without finding fault' and the qualification that the double-minded person 'should not think that he will receive anything from the Lord' (1:5–8)? If not, why not? Put James' logic in your own words.
3. Being careful to note the context, what do you think James means in verse 8 when he describes the doubter as 'unstable in all he does'?
4. Skimming through the rest of James Chapter 1, what exactly do you think James means by the 'high position' (1:9) of the poor believer?
5. In your own words, what exactly is the 'word of truth' (verse 18) and what role does it play in new birth?

4

Doing the Word

James 1:19–27

James 1:19–27 continues the introduction to the book. Just like the first half of the introduction (verses 2–18), each paragraph in this section contains, in miniature, themes that will be explored more fully in Chapters 2– 5. If any distinction is to be made between the first and second half of Chapter 1 it is simply that the section under consideration now increasingly emphasises the need for *action* in the Christian life. The word of God—his wisdom revealed—must be performed not just heard.

ANGER AND HUMILITY (1:19–21)

James 1:19–21 provides a foretaste of a theme to be explored later in the epistle, human anger:

> [19] My dear brothers, take note of this: Everyone should be quick to listen, slow to speak and slow to become angry, [20] for man's anger does not bring about the righteous life that God desires. [21] Therefore, get rid of all moral filth and the evil that is so prevalent and humbly accept the word planted in you, which can save you (1:19–21).

In 3:9–18 and 4:1–3 James will call on his hearers to repent of 'cursing men', harbouring 'bitter envy' and causing 'fights and quarrels'. Here in 1:19–21 he anticipates these themes insisting that wrath toward one another is contrary to the righteous life God desires. The exhortation begins with what appears to be a quotation or allusion to a proverb of some sort: 'take note of this: Everyone should be quick to listen, slow to speak and slow to become angry.' Scholars have sought in vain to find a specific proverbial reference (similar exhortations are found in Prov 13:3; 15:1; 29:20 and in non-biblical Jewish literature from the period). Whatever the specific allusion, James extrapolates in his own words 'for man's anger does not bring about the righteous life that God desires'. The 'anger' here is not a reference to a private emotion; it has to do with how one treats and addresses one's fellow human beings. Anger like this is contrary to the 'righteous' life God wills for us. These ideas pre-empt a dominant theme of the epistle: righteousness/wickedness have to do with relationships. The righteous person is the one who relates rightly to his/her neighbour.

Since God has a specific way of life in mind for the believer, James urges them to get rid of 'moral filth' and 'evil'—in the form of anger toward one another—and to 'humbly accept the word planted in you, which can save you'. Again, the 'moral filth' and 'evil' are almost certainly to be thought of relationally.

The 'word' mentioned here in verse 21 is, of course, the same as the 'word of truth' back in verse 18. In the earlier passage, James emphasised the word's power to give new birth to the believer. Here James stresses the believer's ongoing responsibility to accept that word in the affairs of daily life. God's word not only *gives* life, it also *transforms* life. As the instrument of our new birth, the word fashions us into the family likeness and prepares us for our ultimate salvation. In view of this, says James, we are to 'humble' ourselves before that word. The description of the word as that 'which can save you' is not intended to suggest that obedience to the word wins our salvation—otherwise, it would not be the word which saves but our obedience. James simply wishes to remind his readers that the word of God is not simply something we receive at new birth and then forget about; it is, rather, the very means of our being fitted out for ultimate salvation as we daily 'accept' it in humility.

DOING THE WORD (1:22–25)

The theme of God's 'word' continues on through the next section—indeed, through the entire epistle. Having spoken of the word's power to give new birth (1:18) and of the responsibility of believers to humbly embrace the word in daily life (1:21), James now forthrightly insists that acceptance of the word involves *doing* what it says:

> [22] Do not merely listen to the word, and so deceive yourselves. Do what it says. [23] Anyone who listens to the word but does not do what it says is like a man who looks at his face in a mirror [24] and, after looking at himself, goes away and immediately forgets what he looks like. [25] But the man who looks intently into the perfect law that gives freedom, and continues to do this, not forgetting what he has heard, but doing it—he will be blessed in what he does (1:22–25).

The theme of doing God's will rather than just hearing it will dominate James 2:14–26, one of the most important and controversial sections of the letter. Here, James provides just a teaser for the theme. He offers a somewhat humorous analogy. The person who hears 'the word' (in church presumably) and then fails to put it into practice is like a man who looks in the mirror only to go away and forget immediately what he looks like. We are meant to laugh at this forgetful mirror-gazer and then realise that hearing the word without doing what it says is equally absurd. Not yielding to the word which gave us new birth and which guarantees our salvation is the height of folly.

In verse 25 James describes this word as the 'perfect law that gives freedom'. What exactly does James means by this? Is he talking about the Jewish law (the Torah)? the message of salvation? the New Testament? or something else entirely? Given the train of thought from verse 18 (verses 21, 22, 23) there can be little doubt the 'perfect law' here is roughly synonymous with the 'word of truth' which gives new birth and which is to be humbly accepted in daily life. James then cannot be talking about the Jewish law or about the simple message of salvation. Nor even can he be talking about the New Testament which, for the most part, was written *after* the epistle of James.

There was only one 'word of truth' in the possession of all Christian communities in the middle of the first century: the collection of traditions about the ministry and teaching of Jesus, what scholars call the 'Jesus tradition'. The Jesus tradition was memorised and recounted throughout the churches and later compiled in what we call the four Gospels, all of which were written after the letter of James. These early oral traditions about the Messiah, particularly those recounting Jesus' teaching, are what James means by the 'word of truth' and the 'perfect law'. It is noteworthy also that James regularly alludes in his letter to the very words of Jesus (see the Introduction): James' letter, in fact, could be described as a plea to *do*, not just *HEAR*, the words of Jesus.

But why would James call this body of Jesus-traditions a 'law', a term usually associated with the ancient Jewish Torah. The answer is simple: according to the early Christians, Jesus was the fulfillment of the Torah (Matthew 5:17–18; Luke 24:27; John 5:46; Rom 10:4). He was therefore himself the *new law* (Mark 10:1–12; John 6:32–35; 8:5–11). Like James, the Apostle Paul was happy to speak of the path of Jesus as the '*law* of Christ' (1 Cor 9:21; Gal 6:2). This law, of course, frees us from the judgment of the law of Moses and enables us to please our God, which is why it may be called the law that 'gives freedom' (1:25). A similar thought is found in a saying of Jesus about his teaching:

> 'If you hold to my teaching, you are really my disciples. Then you will know the truth, and the truth will set you free' (John 8:31–32).

Hearing and doing this law, says James at the end of verse 25, is the path of 'blessing': 'he will be blessed in what he does.' The words remind us of Jesus' frequent emphasis on the blessedness of obeying his teaching (Matthew 5:3–11; 11:6; 13:6; 16:17; 24:46; Luke 10:23; 14:13–14):

> As Jesus was saying these things, a woman in the crowd called out, "Blessed is the mother who gave you birth and nursed you." [28] He replied, "Blessed rather are those who *hear* the word of God and *obey* it" (Luke 11:27–28).

The 'blessing' of which James speaks may be eschatological as in 1:12 where the term refers to the 'crown of life' awaiting the faithful. However, the words 'blessed *in what he does*' may suggest a temporal rather than future blessing. In this case, James would perhaps be referring to God's gift of wisdom, i.e. special insight into the paths of God in the midst of trials.

The rest of the epistle will unpack in great detail this path of blessing and obedience to the Messiah's perfect law.

RELIGION AND THE TONGUE (1:26)

Doing the law of Christ involves controlling our speech.

> If anyone considers himself religious and yet does not keep a tight rein on his tongue, he deceives himself and his religion is worthless (1:26).

In keeping with Jesus' own teaching about human speech (Matthew 12:34–37) James will have some very strong things to say about the evil power of words (3:1–12). Here in the introduction, however, he wishes only to flag that our use of the tongue is a key indicator of the value of our religion.

The word 'religion' (thrēskeia), used three times in verses 26–27, is quite rare in the rest of the New Testament (elsewhere only in Acts 26:5 and Col 2:18). Today the term has negative connotations but on James' lips it is a catch-all term for the outward expression of one's faith. Not keeping control of our speech, says James, makes one's expression of faith worthless. The word translated 'worthless' was a very loaded term in James' Jewish tradition. It was a default term for the vacuous 'idols' of pagan worship (1 Kgs 16:13; 2 Kgs 17:15; Ps 24:4; Hos 5:11; Isa 2:20; Isa 44:9; Jer 2:5; Ezek 8:10; Jon 2:8–9, among many others). It is unlikely the first audience will have missed James' point.

RELIGION AND THE POOR (1:27)

Having said what religion is not (verse 26), James in the final sentence of the introduction describes what true religion *is*. And he does so in no uncertain terms.

> Religion that God our Father accepts as pure and faultless is this: to look after orphans and widows in their distress and to keep oneself from being polluted by the world (1:27).

Few passages in the Bible are more forthright than this one about what it is that God 'accepts as pure and faultless'. James does not mean that the activities mentioned in the second half of the verse *make one* (or even one's religion) pure and faultless; he simply means these activities are so important to God that he considers them the perfect outward expression of faith. For James, then, Christian behaviour is epitomised in the twin duties of caring for the world's poor and avoiding the world's perversions. The mention of God as 'father' at the beginning of this verse has a special resonance within the teaching of Jesus (Matthew 6:9) but it is not unusual within Jewish tradition (e.g. Isa 63:16). Indeed, Psalm 68:5 (like James 1:27) connects the fatherhood of God with his care of the fatherless and the widow: 'A father to the fatherless, a defender of widows, is God in his holy dwelling.'

'Orphans and widows' were the archetypal underprivileged in the ancient world. They had few rights, very little power, no status and, without any social welfare system in the Roman empire, they were frequently utterly impoverished. Pure religion, says James, redresses this: it 'looks after' such persons in an effort to ease their distress. The expression 'look after' (*episkeptomai*) can mean either to *visit* or to *care for*. The latter sense is what James has in mind. It connotes personal involvement in meeting the needs of the impoverished. James will give a specific example in Chapter 2:

> Suppose a brother or sister is without clothes and daily food. [16] If one of you says to him, "Go, I wish you well; keep warm and well fed," but does nothing about his physical needs, what good is it? (2:15–16).

The Old Testament is replete with commands similar to that of James (Deut 14:28–29; 24:17–22; Isa 1:15–17; 58:6–7; Jer 5:27–28; Ezek 22:6–7) and the early church continued the practice, caring for the impoverished from the very beginning. In the early AD 30s the Jerusalem church set up a large daily food roster for destitute widows (Acts 6:1– 7). The Apostle Paul instituted a similar program in the Gentile churches (1 Tim 5:3–10). Moreover, in the AD 40s and 50s Paul conducted what was perhaps the world's first truly international aid project, collecting money from the churches of Turkey, Greece and Macedonia for the famine-ravaged believers of Palestine (Rom 15:24–27; 1 Cor 16:1–4; 2 Cor 8–9). Beyond the New Testament period the church of Rome reported that in AD 250 it was supporting 1500 destitute men, women and children daily (Eusebius *Ecclesiastical History* 6.43.11). The early church's care of the poor was inspired not only by Jewish tradition but perhaps especially by Jesus' own teaching (Matthew 25:31–46; Mark 10:21; Luke 10:25–37; 11:41).

Pure religion also keeps 'oneself from being polluted by the world'. James is almost certainly not referring to the pollutions of private immorality (sexual sins, lying, and so on); he means the socio-economic perversions of society. Three things commend this interpretation. Firstly, the reference to the pollutions of the world is deliberately paired with the reference to orphans and widows; in the Greek text there is no 'and' between the two statements. It literally reads: 'Religion that God our Father accepts as pure and faultless is this: to look after orphans and widows in their distress, to keep oneself from being polluted by the world' (1:27). This suggests the two ideas are related. Secondly, the expression 'the world' appears again in Chapter 4 where it has clear financial overtones. Coveting wealth to 'spend what you get on your pleasures' is described by James as 'friendship with *the world*' (4:1–4). Thirdly, immediately following James 1:27 is what appears to be a deliberate example of 'being polluted by the world'—favouring the rich against the poor (2:1–13). The economic dimension of James' words is clear.

In short, James 1:27 insists that contributing to the poor of society and avoiding the socio-economic pollutions of society is the expression of faith God deems acceptable. This two-fold statement at the end of James' introduction to the epistle sets up beautifully the two-fold structure of the first part of the body of the letter (2:1–26). In 2:1–13 James calls for an end to economic favouritism (one of the 'pollutions of the world'). Then, in 2:14–26, he calls for kindness toward the impoverished (i.e. 'looking after widows and orphans').

REFLECTIONS

1. Hearing and doing. James 1:19–27 reminds us that Christian faith is a faith that *works*. First century Judaism was very much a religion of hearing and learning. Central to the life of ancient Jewish life and worship were the Tanakh (our Old Testament) and the 'traditions of the elders', rabbinic rulings about the application of God's law (these rulings were later compiled in the second holy book of Judaism, the Mishnah). These two sources, known as the dual-Torah, were revered, remembered, recalled and rehearsed throughout a pious Jew's life. A problem often associated with a religion of hearing and learning however is that these activities can become goals in themselves. Listening to the Scriptures and memorising their words can be viewed as primary acts of godliness, rather than as the way in which God informs and nourishes the faithful for a life of godliness. James' words remind us that the same problem can be found among the new people of God, those with the new law of the message of Jesus. Advancing in our knowledge of Christ's teaching is not the goal of Christian life; it is the means by which God strengthens us for the life of faith, a faith that works.

2. The central importance of the 'Jesus-tradition'. James 1:19–27 reminds us of the central place of Jesus' own teaching in the life of faith. As pointed out, the 'word of truth' or 'perfect law' which James refers to is none other than the traditions of Jesus. This point will be made over and over throughout the epistle, as James recalls for his readers—sometimes subtly, sometimes obviously—the very words of the Messiah. James reflects a perspective that has marked all apostolic churches throughout the centuries: the foundation of Christian faith is the Jesus-tradition (now) contained in the Gospels. This in no way takes away from the rest of the New Testament; it is simply to underline that the teaching of and about Jesus found in the Gospels provides the basis and background of all subsequent instruction in the New Testament epistles.

3. *Poverty and the Christian.* Caring for 'widows and orphans' is a defining activity of Christian faith, according to James. Throughout the New Testament it is simply assumed that believers will contribute to the poor (Matthew 19:21; Luke 11:41; 12:33; 19:8; Acts 9:36; 10:4; 24:17; Rom 15:26; 2 Cor 8–9; Gal 2:10; 1 John 3:17). There is no controversy over this issue in the New Testament, nor any fear that social welfare might take away from the central mission of the church (to preach the gospel). There is simply an understanding that Christ's love of needy sinners is to be reflected in our love of the materially needy around us. The point is beautifully made, and in a manner deeply resonant with the teaching of James, in one of the letters of the apostle John:

> This is how we know what love is: Jesus Christ laid down his life for us. And we ought to lay down our lives for our brothers. [17] If anyone has material possessions and sees his brother in need but has no pity on him, how can the love of God be in him? [18] Dear children, let us not love with words or tongue but with actions and in truth (1 John 3:16–18).

QUESTIONS FOR DISCUSSION

1. It was suggested above that the 'perfect law that gives freedom' (1:25) and the 'word of truth' (1:18) both refer to the collection of traditions about Jesus' life and teaching (later written down in the Gospels). What is the significance of this observation both for reading James and for the Christian life?
2. Why do you think James describes the word as the law that 'gives freedom' (verse 25)?
3. Why does 'not keeping a tight rein on the tongue' (verse 26) make our religion 'worthless'?
4. James says that caring for the poor and avoiding worldly pollution is the life which God 'accepts as pure and faultless' (verse 27). What do you think James means? In what way does this behaviour make our religion 'pure and faultless'?

5

Worldly Favouritism

James 2:1–13

The economic concerns hinted at in the introduction (1:9–11, 27) receive a sustained treatment in Chapter 2. In 2:1–13 James rebukes those who would dare to favour the rich at the expense of the poor. In 2:14–26 he rebukes those who would dare to assume that 'faith' need not concern itself with the practical needs of the poor. In reverse order, then—as noted in the previous chapter—James deals with the twin topics raised in the climactic verse of the introduction (1:27): the need to care for the destitute and shun the world's pollution.

THE BEST SEATS IN THE HOUSE (2:1–4)

The leading sentences of this section leave us in no doubt as to James' theme:

> My brothers, as believers in our glorious Lord Jesus Christ, don't show favoritism. [2] Suppose a man comes into your meeting wearing a gold ring and fine clothes, and a poor man in shabby clothes also comes in. [3] If you show special attention to the man wearing fine clothes and say, "Here's a good seat for you," but say to the poor man, "You stand there" or "Sit on the floor by my feet," [4] have you not discriminated among yourselves and become judges with evil thoughts? (2:1–4).

The description of Jesus in 2:1 is literally 'our Lord Jesus Christ of the glory'. The intended emphasis here is on the word 'glory'. As noted in the introduction to the commentary, the reference to Jesus' glory probably points to the Lord's resurrection and subsequent position at the right hand of God. Numerous New Testament texts reveal that 'glory' was a default description of the Messiah's exalted existence following his death and resurrection. To the disciples on the road to Emmaus Jesus asks: 'Did not the Christ have to suffer these things and then enter his *glory*?' (Luke 24:26). Throughout his lifetime Jesus frequently spoke of the glory that awaited him in the future: he would sit on a throne of glory (Matthew 19:28; 25:31; Mark 10:37); he would return to judge the world in the Father's glory (Matthew 16:27; Mark 8:38). The Apostle Paul describes Jesus' resurrection body itself (literally) as his 'body of the glory' (Phil 3:21). Given this widespread New Testament tradition, it is likely that James' description of Jesus as the Lord Jesus Christ 'of the glory' is intended to remind readers that the resurrected Messiah sits at God's right hand sharing in the divine rule of the world.

The implied reason for avoiding favouritism is therefore obvious: those who appreciate the glory of Jesus over all things know that all criteria for measuring our *relative* glory are irrelevant. Christians should know better than to measure one another's importance when meeting in the presence of Jesus. 'Gold rings' and 'fine clothes' are meaningless before the riches of Christ's universal majesty. The expression 'believers in' (the glorious Lord Jesus) is literally 'have the faith of/in' and recalls one of the leading themes of the epistle: those who have true faith will show it in their deeds. The point is so obvious to James that he will soon declare that those without good works possess no faith at all (2:14–17).

James offers an example of the kind of favouritism he is talking about. A wealthy man comes into church and is shown a good seat; a poor man enters the building and is told to sit on the floor. The 'good seat' mentioned in verse 3 is not simply the most comfortable one or the one with the best view; it is one of the 'seats of honour' reserved for people of higher social standing. These were commonplace in the ancient world both in banquet halls and in Jewish synagogues. Jesus himself railed against the practice in Jerusalem:

> Beware of the teachers of the law... They love to be greeted in the market-places and have the most important seats in the synagogues and the places of honor at banquets (Luke 20:46).

James 2:1–4 takes Jesus' warning concerning the Jewish leadership in the synagogues of Jerusalem and applies it to the Jewish-Christian meetings throughout the Diaspora. In fact, the word translated 'meeting' in verse 2 ('Suppose a man comes into your *meeting*') is *sunagōgē*, literally 'synagogue'. The word may simply be intended to jog readers' memories of the particular saying of Jesus quoted above. Alternatively, it may provide evidence that Jewish-Christians in this period continued to describe their church gatherings using traditional Jewish vocabulary. In any case, Christian congregations, says James, must not emulate Jewish congregations in providing socially-graded seating. Christians must avoid the pollution of the world at this point and determine never to show favouritism toward the rich.

The assessment of favouritism in verse 4 is forceful: 'have you not discriminated among yourselves and become judges with evil thoughts?' (2:4). In modern English the word 'evil' is typically reserved for the worst kind of people, not for those who simply favour the rich. This says as much about modern culture as it does the message of James. In the opinion of James (following Jesus), few things are more repugnant than *esteeming wealth at the expense of relationships*. And 'favouritism' is a classic example of just that. As much as it grates with modern sensibilities, showing favouritism is in biblical terms 'evil'. The criticism about being 'judges', evil ones at that, is compounded when one remembers, as James will later affirm: 'There is only one Lawgiver and Judge, the one who is able to save and destroy. But you—who are you to judge your neighbour?' (4:12).

James goes on to offer his reasons for using such strong language.

RHETORICAL QUESTIONS ABOUT POOR AND RICH (2:5–7)

In verses 5–7 James fires off a series of rhetorical questions designed to underscore the absurdity of Christians showing favouritism to the wealthy:

> 5 Listen, my dear brothers: Has not God chosen those who are poor in the eyes of the world to be rich in faith and to inherit the kingdom he promised those who love him?
> 6 But you have insulted the poor. Is it not the rich who are exploiting you? Are they not the ones who are dragging you into court?
> 7 Are they not the ones who are slandering the noble name of him to whom you belong?

James begins by addressing his hearers as 'dear', literally 'beloved'. As scathing as James is about those who would favour the rich and ignore the poor, he speaks out of love and concern for fellow members of God's family.

The first question about God having 'chosen the poor ... to inherit the kingdom' recalls the statement of Jesus: 'Blessed are you who are poor, for yours is the kingdom of God' (Luke 6:20). While Matthew's version of the saying leaves the financial meaning of 'poor' unclear ('poor in spirit', Matthew 5:3), Luke's contrast between the 'blessed poor' and the 'cursed rich' leaves us in no doubt ('But woe to you who are rich, for you have already received your comfort.'" Luke 6:24). It is because his readers know this saying of Jesus (probably in its Lukan form) that James can pose his point as a rhetorical question: 'Has not God chosen those who are poor?' The first readers would have to answer: yes, indeed, our Lord said exactly this.

Verse 5 reflects not only Jesus' teaching but also the historical reality. James is pointing out what everyone in his audience knew. With a few notable exceptions, the first Christians came from among the socially poor: not the poverty-stricken class of slaves and beggars but the great mass of people one step above them—artisans, farmers, fishermen and so on. God chose to reach the world not from the top down but from the bottom up. The Apostle Paul said something similar (1 Cor 1:26–29). How tragic and ironic, then, argues James, that believers would favour the rich and 'insult the poor'. 'Insult' here in verse 6 is the Greek verb *atimazō* which literally means *to dishonour.* James does not mean that Christians are maligning the poor, verbally or otherwise; he means that by favouring the rich over the poor these Christians have effectively stripped the poor of the honour shown to them by God and his Messiah.

The irony continues through verses 6–7. You show favouritism to the rich, says James, when you know very well they are the ones 'exploiting you', 'dragging you into court' and 'slandering the name' of Jesus? The Greek of these verses (as well as the English) shifts to using present tense verbs: dragging, exploiting, slandering. James is not necessarily arguing that the rich *always* do such things; he is pointing out what the wealthy of society were doing at the time he wrote his letter.

'Exploiting' (*katadunasteuō*) has financial overtones and frequently appears in the ancient Greek translation of the Old Testament (known as the Septuagint), from which James often cites, in the context of the rich 'oppressing' the poor (1 Sam 12:3; Jer 7:6; Ezek 18:12, 22:29; Hos 12:7; Amos 4:1, 8:4; Mic 2:2; Zech 7:10; Mal 3:5). James will give a concrete example of the rich oppressing/exploiting the poor in 5:1–6.

The 'courts' into which these Christians are being 'dragged' (*elkō*, a strong verb in Greek) may be either civil courts or synagogue courts. On what charges Christians are being taken to court, whether religious or civil, is not stated. And we may not need to choose between the two. It is easy to envisage trumped up civil charges motivated by religious differences.

'Slandering' (*blasphēmeō*) is the technical term for *blaspheming* and, no doubt, James intends to suggest this religious connotation. Those who revile Jesus Christ are not simply insulting an equal; they are blaspheming the glorious Lord who sits at God's right hand.

THE LAW OF LOVE (2:8–11)

James drives home his message with a theological observation about the nature of God's law:

> [8] If you really keep the royal law found in Scripture, "Love your neighbour as yourself," you are doing right. [9] But if you show favouritism, you sin and are convicted by the law as law-breakers (2:8–9).

Showing favouritism (which is still the topic under consideration) breaks the fundamental command of God's word: the command to love. The specific law quoted in verse 8 comes from Leviticus 19:18: 'love your neighbour as yourself.' Why does James call this command the 'royal' law? There is nothing in the text of Leviticus, or in the history of Judaism, which suggests a royal connotation of this specific commandmentt.

The answer is probably to be found in the observation that Leviticus 19:18 had peculiar significance for Jesus, the descendent of King David and glorious Messiah who inaugurated the Kingdom of God. So far as we can tell, Leviticus 19:18 was accorded no special status in Jewish thought beyond its place among the 613 commandments of Jewish Scripture (by the count of the Pharisees). Jesus, however, insisted that this one sentence summarised the entire will of God for our treatment of one another (Mark 12:31). As the Messiah, he declared that love (of God and neighbour) was the demand upon which 'all the Law and the Prophets hang'. Instantly, then, Leviticus 19:18 was elevated to 'royal' status. 'Showing favouritism', says James, is a repudiation of a command which Jesus, the true King, brought into the centre of kingdom living. It is easy to see how 'showing favouritism' *breaks* this royal law. If I am kinder to the wealthy than I am to the poor, it is clear that I do not love both rich and poor as I love myself. I am therefore a 'lawbreaker' or transgressor, one who throws off the yoke of God's will.

The theological argument continues in verse 10:

> 10 For whoever keeps the whole law and yet stumbles at just one point is guilty of breaking all of it. 11 For he who said, "Do not commit adultery," also said, "Do not murder." If you do not commit adultery but do commit murder, you have become a law-breaker (2:10–11).

Why are adultery and murder introduced into a discussion about favouritism? The answer appears to be as follows. To illustrate the fact that breaking the royal law of Leviticus 19:18 makes one an official 'law-breaker', James demonstrates the same principle from two of the most famous and dramatic commandments in the Scriptures: the sixth and seventh commandments (Exodus 20:13–14) of the famous Ten Commandments. If someone faithfully keeps the law about adultery, says James, and yet breaks the one about murder, such a person is hardly a keeper of the law; rather he is 'law-breaker'. He has defied the God from whose mouth both commandments came. Everyone in James' audience would agree with this line of reasoning. How much more, then, runs James' underlying logic, does this principle apply to the command elevated to royal status by the Messiah himself. I could keep every other law in the Scriptures, but if I refused to love my neighbour as myself, it would count for nothing. I would be a 'law-breaker', says James, and no amount of other law-keeping will obscure that.

Other factors may also lie in the background of James' argument. In 4:1–4 James will equate financial disobedience with murder and adultery:

> 1 What causes fights and quarrels among you? Don't they come from your desires that battle within you? 2 You want something but don't get it. You kill and covet, but you cannot have what you want. You quarrel and fight. You do not have, because you do not ask God. 3 When you ask, you do not receive, because you ask with wrong motives, that you may spend what you get on your pleasures. 4 You adulterous people, don't you know that friendship with the world is hatred towards God? (James 4:1–4).

Elsewhere in the New Testament, neglect or hatred of the poor is equated with 'murder' (1 John 3:15–17). Hence, the references to adultery and murder here in James 2:11–12 may have the double meaning of connoting the spiritual murder and adultery which is neglect of the needy. Showing favouritism toward the rich, then, is cast by James in a very serious light.

LIVING IN LIGHT OF THE JUDGMENT (2:12–13)

James concludes his discussion of the economic pollution which is favouritism with a stark call to right behaviour in the face of the coming judgement:

> 12 Speak and act as those who are going to be judged by the law that gives freedom, 13 because judgment without mercy will be shown to anyone who has not been merciful. Mercy triumphs over judgment! (James 2:12–13).

Believers are to behave as those who will be judged according to the 'law that gives freedom'. As in 1:25, this phrase refers to the traditions about Jesus, God's new law. This fits well with the observation (just made) that the command to love is given its *royal* status precisely because of its central place in the message of Jesus. In short, then, the lives of Christians are to be weighed against Jesus' teaching, the central and organising principle of which is the obligation to love one another. Numerous passages in the Gospels describe Jesus' teaching as the criterion of future judgment (Matthew 7:21–27; Matthew 25:31–46; Luke 11:31–32). Of course, this is not to imply salvation by works—James 1:17–18 has already made clear that new birth is a gift—but it is to underscore the fact that works are the proof of new birth: a good tree produces good fruit (Luke 6:43). This is a theme James will take up in earnest in the second half of Chapter 2.

James' reliance upon the teaching of Jesus continues into verse 13. The idea that divine mercy is somehow related to human mercy comes straight out of the Sermon on the Mount: 'Blessed are the merciful, for they will be shown mercy' (Matthew 5:7). What Jesus put positively, James recasts into a warning about what happens to those who have not been merciful. Mercy is so fundamental to God's nature, insists James, that to refuse acts of mercy to another is to prove myself an unbeliever, a person under judgment.

But how is being 'merciful' related to the issue of showing favouritism to the rich? The basic meaning of the Greek word 'mercy' (*eleos*) is *pity* or *compassion* which is why, when used of God, it tends to refer to forgiveness, his willingness to have pity on sinners. When used of human behaviour, however, *mercy* very frequently refers not to our forgiveness of one another but to our 'charity/generosity' toward the needy. The central Old and New Testament expression for what we today would call 'charity' (kindness to the poor) is literally *to do mercy*. The NIV usually translates the expression 'almsgiving' or 'give to the needy' but the underlying Greek root is 'mercy' (Matthew 6:2, 3, 4; Luke 11:41; 12:33; Acts 3:2, 3, 10; 9:36; 10:2, 4; 10:31; 24:17).

The thought is captured well in Jesus' parable of the Good Samaritan. Interestingly, the parable itself is an explanation to a Jewish rabbi of what it means to 'love your neighbour as yourself' (Luke 10:27–29), to obey the royal law, in other words. After contrasting the actions of Jewish leaders with the generosity of a passing Samaritan, Jesus concludes:

> 36 Which of these three do you think was a neighbour to the man who fell into the hands of robbers? 37 The expert in the law replied, "The one who *had mercy* (*eleos*) on him." Jesus told him, "Go and do likewise" (Luke 10:36–37).

This is the understanding of 'mercy' which stands behind James' teaching in Chapter 2: indeed, the expression 'to do mercy' (*poiein eleos*) is exactly the same in both Luke 10:37 and James 2:13. It would not be at all surprising if James had Jesus' parable in mind throughout this section. In any case, the combination of themes (love of neighbour, rich and poor, showing mercy) is very similar. Shaming the poor in favour of the rich is to withhold pity from those in need and will result, says James, in God withholding his pity from us at the judgement.

It is in this context that James delivers his final and dramatic statement on the subject: 'Mercy triumphs over judgment!' (2:13). Unfortunately, the English word 'triumph' no longer provides the best translation of the Greek term (*katakauchaomai*). Nowadays, to triumph means 'to gain a victory'. The *Oxford English Dictionary*, however, offers a second, older meaning: 'rejoice or exult at a victory.' This is the meaning in James 2:13. The Greek term means to exult or boast in victory not to *achieve* the victory. In fact, in James 3:14 the term is translated simply 'boast': 'But if you harbour bitter envy and selfish ambition in your hearts, do not *boast*' (3:14).

What, then, does James mean when he says that mercy will exult/boast over judgement? One interpretation takes 'mercy' here to refer to God's mercy. James would then be saying that on the Day of Judgment God's mercy will be exultant because we who deserved judgement for our failures (to be merciful) will nonetheless find ourselves saved by God's mercy. The interpretation is attractive because of the comfort it potentially offers to the reader. However it almost certainly runs counter to James' intention and contradicts his insistence (in the previous sentence) that those who have not been merciful will receive judgement *without* mercy.

A second interpretation is preferable. The 'mercy' which 'exults' over judgement is in fact *our* mercy toward others, our pity toward the needy (as in the Parable of the Good Samaritan). This does not mean that human mercy will *gain* the victory over divine judgement, only that such mercy will have cause to boast in that victory on the last day. Why? Because those who 'do mercy' in this life show themselves thereby to be true recipients of God's mercy. Human mercy is the proof of having received divine mercy. Mercy is so fundamental to the life of God's people that it is the sign of who those people are. Of course, as I said before, this is nothing other than the teaching of Jesus: 'Blessed are the merciful, for they will be shown mercy' (Matthew 5:7). Precisely the same logic is present in Matthew 25:31–46, a passage worthy of deep reflection on the part of the modern church.

REFLECTIONS

1. Favouritism and Christ's majesty. Avoiding 'favouritism' is not an expression of a mere liberal humanism, being good to each other for goodness sake. The issue raised by James in 2:1–13 cuts to the heart of what it means to believe in 'our glorious Lord Jesus Christ'. When we understand Christ's majesty over all, and begin to view the world from that lofty perspective, making distinctions based on wealth, or clothes, or status—or anything else—becomes farcical and, worse, a betrayal of the only truly glorious one, the one who crystallised what it means to follow him in the words of his royal law: 'Love your neighbour as yourself'.

2. The test of love. The central place given by James to the royal law of love is striking. The test of Christian health is how one treats one's neighbour. The same perspective can be found in Paul: 'Love does no harm to its neighbour. Therefore love is the fulfilment of the law' (Rom 13:10); 'And now these three remain: faith, hope and love. But the greatest of these is love' (1 Cor 13:13); 'The only thing that counts is faith expressing itself through love' (Gal 5:6); 'The entire law is summed up in a single command: "Love your neighbour as yourself"' (Gal 5:14). Or as the Apostle John would later write: 'And this is his [God's] command: to believe in the name of his Son, Jesus Christ, and to love one another as he [Jesus] commanded us' (1 John 3:23). The impact of Jesus' emphasis on Lev 19:18 was felt everywhere in early Christianity. The witness of James, and of the wider New Testament, suggests that only one true test of vitality exists for the followers of the Messiah: obedience to his royal command, 'Love your neighbour as yourself'.

QUESTIONS FOR DISCUSSION

1. In 2:1 James describes Jesus as 'our glorious Lord Jesus Christ' (which is literally, 'the Lord Jesus Christ of the glory'). Unpack in your own words exactly what you think James means by this description. What does Jesus' glory consist of?

2. Read 2:5–7 again. Is Christianity biased against the rich? Why/why not?
3. What is the significance of describing the command to love as 'the royal law' (2:8)? Why is this command, above everything else the Bible teaches, *royal*?
4. There is a lot of talk in these verses about keeping the law and breaking the law. Is this legalistic? Why/why not?
5. Read the Parable of the Good Samaritan (Luke 10:25– 37). What connections can you see between this parable and the teaching of James in 2:8–13?

6

Faith and Works, Rich and Poor

James 2:14–26

The reference to 'doing mercy' (= charity) in James 2:13 provides a clever transition from one section to the next: it concludes James' teaching about our treatment of the rich (2:1–12) and introduces his teaching about our treatment of the poor (2:14–26).

James 2:14–26 is sometimes read as a treatise on the theology of 'faith and works', as if James' main concern here were a doctrinal one. The introductory scenario described in verses 15–16 (a Christian's neglect of the poor) is thus interpreted as a mere illustration of a broader theological argument. In what follows, however, I hope to show that this reading is mistaken. The way James has been building the economic theme ever since 1:27 should alert us to the fact that far from being a kind of sermon illustration, the situation described in 2:15–16 is what this portion of the letter is all about. Christians had not only been favouring the rich (2:1–13), they had been withholding mercy from the poor. The 'purity' and 'faultlessness' of their religion (1:27) was in serious question; or, to put it in the language of 2:14– 26, their 'faith' was in danger of being worthless.

As we explore James' compelling argument about faith and works we would do well to recall the very practical situation these words seek to redress. What theology there is in this passage is intended to motivate readers to perform the particular kinds of works implied in 2:15–16.

THE CONTROVERSY OF JAMES 2:14–26

James 2:14–26 is the most controversial passage in the Book of James. In fact, in some circles James 2:14–26 would be regarded as the most problematic portion of the entire New Testament. I said in the introduction that the great sixtheenth century Reformer, Martin Luther, regarded James as an 'epistle of straw'. He did so largely on the basis of statements in the second half of Chapter 2. Luther believed that James' teaching contradicted that of Paul on the question of saving faith. Paul taught:

> For it is by grace you have been saved, through faith—and this not from yourselves, it is the gift of God—not by works, so that no-one can boast (Ephesians 2:8–9).

James, however, taught:

> You see that a person is justified by what he does and not by faith alone (James 2:24).

Since Paul's thought is more widely attested in the New Testament than that of James, the letter of James had to go. Such was the logic of Luther in the heat of his battle with a medieval church which taught that good works, especially in the form of financial gifts (to the church), could atone for certain sins of both you and your family members.

Luther's decision to sideline the letter of James was, as later Reformers pointed out, based on two mistakes: insufficient attention to the context of Paul's message and a fundamental misreading of the teaching of James. To Gentiles fearful that one could not be saved by the Jewish Messiah without becoming a Jew oneself, Paul rightly insisted that salvation is based not on fulfilling the works of the Old Testament but by placing one's faith in Jesus Christ. When Paul said this, however, he never envisaged that a wedge could be driven between trusting Jesus and obeying Jesus. Works of love (the 'royal law') were always the fundamental expression of what Paul meant by 'faith'. The thought is captured beautifully in the words of Galatians 5:6:

> For in Christ Jesus neither circumcision nor uncircumcision has any value. The only thing that counts is faith expressing itself through love.

To believe in Christ—note: 'belief' and 'faith' are the same word in Greek—is not merely to agree that Jesus lived, died and rose again; it is to trust him as Lord of your life. Thus, implicit to Paul's doctrine of salvation through faith in Christ is the expectation that one will live in accordance with the will of the Lord—to love your neighbour as yourself. What else would trusting the Lord mean than devoting yourself to his wishes. In Paul's thought, then, 'faith' is always connected to 'good works' not because these two things together save you but because faith entails good works inasmuch as it consists in trusting the One who called on us to love our neighbours (see Eph 2:8–10; Titus 3:4–8).

The critical thing to hold in mind as we approach James 2:14–26 is that the brother of the Lord is doing battle with believers who hold that it *is* possible to have 'faith' in God and Jesus without a commitment to the path of love. James addresses not nervous Gentiles who fear that justification comes through performing the works of the Jewish Law, but presumptuous Jews who suppose that justification comes on the basis of mere *assent* to God and his Messiah, and that devotion to the Messiah's royal law of love is an optional extra. This fact accounts for the apparent tension between Paul's and James' teaching.

THE PERVERSION OF FAITH (2:14–19)

James immediately highlights the corrupt nature of the 'faith' of some in his audience:

> What good is it, my brothers, if a man claims to have faith but has no deeds? Can such faith save him? [14] What good is it, my brothers, if a man claims to have faith but has no deeds? Can such faith save him? [15] Suppose a brother or sister is without clothes and daily food. [16] If one of you says to him, "Go, I wish you well; keep warm and well fed," but does nothing about his physical needs, what good is it? [17] In the same way, faith by itself, if it is not accompanied by action, is dead. [18] But someone will say, "You have faith; I have deeds." Show me your faith without deeds, and I will show you my faith by what I

> do. 19 You believe that there is one God. Good! Even the demons believe that—and shudder (2:14–19).

The opening line (verse 14) sets the scene for our interpretation of the entire passage. The critical thing to note is that James does not consider this hypothetical Christian to have *true* faith. The man merely 'claims to have faith'. The reference in the next clause to '*such* faith' makes clear that, in James' view, the 'faith' now under discussion is merely a version of faith or, more correctly, a perversion of faith. It involves a definition quite unlike that normally used by James and Paul. Up to this point James has been happy to use the word 'faith/believe' as a default description of Christian devotion (1:3; 1:6; 2:1; 2:5). Now, however, he gives up his preferred meaning in order to argue with his readers using their own terms.

On the lips of James' addressees the word 'faith' means something like 'assent', a mere conviction about the truth of God. This is clear not only from the separation of 'faith' from 'deeds' in the opening line but especially from the words of verse 19: 'You believe ('have faith') that there is one God. Good! Even the demons believe that—and shudder.' The 'belief', or 'faith', of this person is not a true trust in God and his Messiah but a mere intellectual conviction that there is just one God, the foundational doctrine of ancient Judaism.

The reference to 'one God' recalls the Shema, the creed which Orthodox Jews to modern times recite twice daily: 'Hear [Hebrew: *shema*], O Israel: The LORD is our God, the LORD, the One and Only (Deut 6:4)[1]. As strange as it sounds to modern ears, the Jewish Christians with whom James takes issue in this passage held that assent to 'monotheism'—the mere recitation of the Shema—was a magical guarantee of salvation regardless of how one behaved. Interestingly, a similar attitude on the part of first century Jews is observable in Romans 2:1–4, 13, 17–29.

---

1. The translation of the Shema quoted here comes from the Jewish prayer book (The Complete Artscroll Siddur. New York: Mesorah Publications, 2003, p.91).

James begs to differ, and throughout these verses he offers four stinging criticisms of this so called 'faith'. Firstly, he insists that such faith is powerless to save. In a question which implies a negative answer verse 14 asks: 'Can such faith save him?' Mere assent that there is one God (or that Jesus is Messiah) is not saving faith.

Secondly, in verses 15–17 James insists that a faith which blesses the poor but performs no deeds of mercy is in fact 'dead'. In the scenario offered here the believer does have some feeling toward the needy. He says to the hungry and clothes-less brother or sister, 'Go, I wish you well'. These words imply not just a physical concern but a spiritual one as well. The phrase is literally, 'May you go in peace'. It recalls a traditional Jewish departure blessing: 'God's peace be upon you'. 'Peace' (*shalom* in Hebrew) is a catch-all term; it denotes the whole range of God's blessings. The problem is: true faith is not a mere sentiment. Without deeds of mercy 'faith' is dead.

Thirdly, James rebukes his readers for supposing that one can separate faith from deeds. In verse 18 he introduces a hypothetical questioner: 'But someone will say, "You have faith; I have deeds"'. If the questioner were attacking James directly we might have expected the statement to be put the other way around: 'You (James) have deeds; I (opponent) have faith.' But it is probably simpler to imagine that the interlocutor's words are a generalised speculation about the possibility of any two Christians emphasising *either* faith *or* deeds (the 'you' and 'I', then, are simply rhetorical). Perhaps the interlocutor thinks of deeds of mercy, such as that demanded by James, as a spiritual calling demanded only of some. 'Showing mercy/charity' is elsewhere described as a particular gift (Rom 12:8). Whatever the case, James make clear in verse 18b that any separation of emphasis is impossible. Deeds (of mercy) are not a Christian option; they are the proof of true faith.

Fourthly and climactically, deedless faith, says James in verse 19, is the faith of demons: 'You believe that there is one God. Good! Even the demons believe that—and shudder.' There may be a rhetorical jibe here: unlike some in James' readership, at least demons know to *shudder* in their knowledge of God.

EXAMPLES OF TRUE FAITH (2:20–26)

From verse 20 onwards, James offers 'evidence that faith without deeds is useless', and he begins the section with a rebuke: 'You foolish man.' The use of the singular ('man'), as opposed to the typical epistolary plural ('brothers': 2:1, 5, 14), suggests James is engaging in a rhetorical device known as diatribe. Here, then, James is continuing a hypothetical debate with an imaginary detractor. James' readers are to listen in to the debate and find themselves addressed in a second-hand way as James demolishes the assumptions of his interlocutor. Paul uses the same rhetorical style in Romans 2:17–24 and for a strikingly similar purpose.

Unlike the scenario of 2:15–16 which describes the actual deeds of faith James wants his audience to perform, the examples of Abraham (2:21–24) and Rahab (2:25–26) are illustrations of the theological point. First: Abraham.

> 21 Was not our ancestor Abraham considered righteous for
> what he did when he offered his son Isaac on the altar?
> 22 You see that his faith and his actions were working
> together, and his faith was made complete by what he
> did. 23 And the scripture was fulfilled that says, "Abraham
> believed God, and it was credited to him as righteousness,"
> and he was called God's friend (2:21–23).

In Genesis 15:6, the first book of the Old Testament, Abraham, the first Jew is said to have 'believed God'. This 'belief' (faith) was credited to him as 'righteousness'. But was the faith of Abraham a deedless faith such as that assumed among James' hearers? No. Every reader of the Old Testament knew that Abraham's faith expressed itself in the most striking deed imaginable: offering his own son to God (Gen 22:1–19). Abraham's faith was not a mere conviction about the reality of the one true God; it was a conviction which, in the words of verse 22, was 'made complete,' that is, revealed to be *true* faith, by his act of devotion.

Abraham's act of devotion in Genesis 22 was the fulfilment, says James, of the declaration in Genesis 15:6 about Abraham's faith. James writes: 'And the scripture was fulfilled that says, "Abraham believed God".' In other words, the thing which fulfilled the description of Abraham as a true believer in God (*believer* in the true sense) was not a mere deedless assent but an active devotion. To 'believe in God', in the scriptural sense, argues James, entails a commitment to action. Thus, in the words of verse 24, a person is justified by 'what he does' inasmuch as this demonstrates the presence of true faith. 'Faith alone' does not justify, for faith which is alone is no faith at all. Again, when James states here that 'faith alone' does not justify he is using the word 'faith' in the truncated way his readers had been employing the term, not in his preferred manner (the manner of Genesis 15:6).

James continues in verses 25–26 to make exactly the same point from another, more minor, Old Testament character, Rahab the prostitute (Joshua 2):

> In the same way, was not even Rahab the prostitute considered righteous for what she did when she gave lodging to the spies and sent them off in a different direction?

Moving from the founding father of Judaism to a pagan harlot is hardly a climactic form of argumentation—unless, of course, James is making a similar point to that made in 2:19. Demons tremble in the knowledge that there is one God, which is more than can be said for some in James' audience. Rahab's recognition of the one true God moved her to show hospitality to the Jewish spies and to help them escape Jericho without harm. James may have wanted to imply that demons and pagan prostitutes have a better grasp of saving faith than some in his readership. The fact that Rahab gave lodging to those in need may also have made her relevant given the scenario of 2:15–16.

James concludes the discussion with a pithy simile illustrating his central point: 'As the body without the spirit is dead, so faith without deeds is dead' (2:26). James is probably thinking of the creation narrative in Genesis wherein God breathes his breath/spirit into the body of Adam 'and the man became a living being' (2:7). The comparison must not be taken too far. James does not mean that deeds animate faith just as the spirit animates the body. He simply means that just as physical life consists of body + spirit, so spiritual life consists of faith + deeds.

REFLECTION

1. *Love for the poor.* James 2:14–26 seeks to apply the royal law of love to a particular area of Christian conduct—care for the poor. From 1:27 James has sought to impress upon his readers the nature of acceptable religion, or true faith. It shuns the world's bias toward the rich (2:1–13) and strives to show mercy toward the poor (2:14–26). As I said earlier, 2:15–16 is not a mere analogy designed to highlight a theological point; it is rather the reason for the entire discussion. Christians had been ignoring the plight of the needy. Christian sentiment toward the poor is not enough, says James. Faith will show itself in providing for those who lack food and clothes. Otherwise, it will show itself not to be true faith at all. The apostle John writes about a similar matrix of ideas:

> If anyone has material possessions and sees his brother in need but has no pity on him, how can the love of God be in him? Dear children, let us not love with words or tongue but with actions and in truth (1 John 3:17–18).

2. *World poverty today.* According to the World Bank, 1.2 billion people in the world right now live on less than a dollar a day. The U.N. *Food and Agriculture Organisation Report* (2003) calculated that over 68,000 people a day die of starvation in the modern world. To combat poverty governments around the world assign a portion of their Gross National Income (GNI = GDP) to Overseas Aid and Development (OAD). In Australia that portion for the 2006–07 budget is 0.3% of GNI. And while Australia provides more (in percentage terms) than some in the OECD (Organisation for Economic Cooperation and Development), it provides less than a great number of those 30 nations, including New Zealand, the UK, France and Ireland. Denmark, for instance, gives 1% of GNI to Overseas Aid and Development—four times our percentage figure. The point of understanding these figures is that Christians simply cannot rely on their taxes to redress world poverty. The reality is: the amount going from our taxes to

the world's poor is miniscule. If a household is paying, say, $20,000 tax a year, only $60 of that is going to overseas aid. In light of the contemporary reality, the words of James are probably more applicable today than in any other period of Christian history: 'What good is it, my brothers, if a man claims to have faith but has no deeds?'

QUESTIONS FOR DISCUSSION

1. Read 2:14 again. What connections can you seen between this verse and what James has said so far in the epistle?
2. Summarise in your own words the version of 'faith' James is criticising in 2:14–19. How does it compare to true faith?
3. In your own words, what exactly does James mean when he says 'his (Abraham's) faith was made complete by what he did' (verse 22)?
4. Read Ephesians 2:8–10. What response would you give to the charge that James 2:24 contradicts the teaching of Paul?
5. How would you describe the purpose of 2:20–26 within the epistle of James as a whole?

7

Mere Words?

James 3:1–12

The old adage 'Sticks and stones may break my bones but words can never harm me' is more memorable than it is true. Most of us will be able to recall occasions when words carried a force far beyond that of sticks and stones. James flagged the power of words in the introduction to the letter: 'If anyone considers himself religious and yet does not keep a tight rein on his tongue, he deceives himself and his religion is worthless' (1:26). This theme now receives full and forceful treatment in Chapter 3.

A WARNING TO WOULD-BE TEACHERS (3:1)

James begins with a strong warning to those who would presume to use their tongue to teach other Christians:

> Not many of you should presume to be teachers, my brothers, because you know that we who teach will be judged more strictly (3:1).

'Teachers' in early Christianity performed a role critical to the survival of the church. In a period of low literacy (10– 15%), teachers were the ones entrusted with memorising and passing on the traditions about Jesus as laid down by the original apostles. Before these traditions were codified in what we call the Gospels and the letters of the New Testament, a believer's only reliable access to what Jesus and the apostles said and did was through the teachers. The thought is captured well in the Apostle Paul's instructions to Timothy about the need to preserve the apostolic words:

> And the things you have heard me say in the presence of many witnesses entrust to reliable men who will also be qualified to teach others (2 Tim 2:2).

If a congregation wanted to recall what Jesus had said about, say, violence or revenge, the teacher would be ready with a quotation from the memorised tradition: 'turn the other cheek', 'Blessed are the peace-makers', and so on. If the church wanted to reflect again on the significance of Jesus' death, the teacher would be able to remind people of what was passed on to them by the apostles: 'This cup is the new covenant in my blood.'

The role of the teacher, then, especially before the completion of the New Testament, was pivotal to the spiritual health of a congregation. An exaggeration here or an omission there had the potential to lead a congregation away from the apostolic foundation.

Teaching was serious business, which is why James warns that 'not many' should presume to take up the role. Of course, the phrase 'not many' implies that a few will and should. However, they should do so in the knowledge that with such a grave responsibility comes stricter judgment. The notion that degrees of judgement are somehow connected to degrees of responsibility reflects Jesus' own instruction (Luke 12:47–48; Matthew 11:20–24). In fact, Jesus himself warned that the teachers of his own day were likely to 'receive greater judgement' (literal translation of Mark 12:40). The wording is almost identical to that in James 3:1. That James' audience knew this saying of Jesus may be suggested by the words '*you know* that we who teach will be judged more strictly'.

STUMBLING PERFECTLY (3:2)

But how does this warning to would-be teachers relate to the theme of speech-ethics which occupies 3:2–12? The answer is quite simple. The presence of some in his audience who wanted to become congregational speakers provides James with a perfect opportunity to discuss a theme relevant not only to teachers but also to believers generally—the need to control the tongue:

> We all stumble in many ways. If anyone is never at fault in what he says, he is a perfect man, able to keep his whole body in check (3:2).

The NIV translation of this verse leaves an overly unrealistic impression of what James says. Firstly, the expression 'is never at fault in what he says' is literally just '*is not stumbling* in what he says'. For aesthetic reasons, the translators may have wanted to avoid repeating the word 'stumble' from the preceding sentence. Secondly, the verb 'stumble' appears in the present tense and probably has a continuous sense. In other words, the expectation is not that we would *not once stumble*; it is rather that we would *not go on stumbling*. This may still sound difficult enough.

The word 'perfect' may also be misleading in this context. Today, the word 'perfect' in a moral context usually conjures up notions of scoring 10/10, of being 'sinless'. This is not a necessary meaning even of the English. The *Oxford English Dictionary* gives three meanings, one of which closely corresponds to the Greek term used by James: (1) 'complete', (2) 'faultless' and (3) 'very satisfactory' (as in 'a perfect evening'). The Greek word *teleios* in verse 2 means something like 'complete'; it does not mean faultless. This is why biblical translators usually opt for a word like 'whole' or 'mature' when rendering this Greek term. James 1:4 offers a *perfect* example: 'Perseverance must finish its work so that you may be *mature*' (*teleios*).

The upshot of all this is to say that James 3:2 is not quite as unrealistic and hypothetical as the NIV translation implies. James is simply saying that although we all stumble in a variety of ways, those who gain control over what they say are *mature* Christians—well on their way to mastering their entire ethical life: 'able to keep his whole body in check.' 'Body' frequently connotes not just the physical dimension of a person but the entire person. This is James' meaning here.

How we speak to others, then, is a kind of barometer of the whole of life. It may seem like a secondary issue but, in the opinion of James, speech is one of the most potent dimensions of our moral existence. In this regard, James echoes the message of his brother:

> [33] Make a tree good and its fruit will be good, or make a tree bad and its fruit will be bad, for a tree is recognised by its fruit. [34] You brood of vipers, how can you who are evil say anything good? For out of the overflow of the heart the mouth speaks. [35] The good man brings good things out of the good stored up in him, and the evil man brings evil things out of the evil stored up in him. [36] But I tell you that men will have to give account on the day of judgment for every careless word they have spoken. [37] For by your words you will be acquitted, and by your words you will be condemned (Matthew 12:33–37).

James 3:1–12 appears to be an extended reflection on this particular teaching of Jesus. This becomes more apparent when we compare Jesus' introduction to this theme ('a tree is recognised by its fruit' Matthew 12:33) with James' conclusion ('can a fig tree bear olives, or a grapevine bear figs?' James 3:12). We will look more closely at these connections later.

SIMILES AND METAPHORS OF THE TONGUE (3:3–8)

James drives his point home with two evocative similes:

> [3] When we put bits into the mouths of horses to make them obey us, we can turn the whole animal. [4] Or take ships as an example. Although they are so large and are driven by strong winds, they are steered by a very small rudder wherever the pilot wants to go. [5] Likewise the tongue is a small part of the body, but it makes great boasts (3:3–5a).

One might gain the impression from these first two illustrations that James thinks the tongue actually controls the rest of our life, just as a 'bit' turns a horse and a rudder steers a ship. However, that would be to turn similes into allegories. James tells us in verse 5 the simple point he wishes to draw from these illustrations: a small instrument can produce a large effect. The particular effect James names in verse 5 is 'boasting'. The reference here is probably not to what we might call personal 'bragging' but to speech which belittles or lords it over others.

The third illustration, this time a metaphor, describes the tongue in thoroughly negative terms:

> 5b Consider what a great forest is set on fire by a small spark. 6 The tongue also is a fire, a world of evil among the parts of the body. It corrupts the whole person, sets the whole course of his life on fire, and is itself set on fire by hell (James 3:5b–6).

An apparently small comment—a lie, an insult, a piece of gossip—can set on fire the entire course of one's life. It can damage relationships, destroy trust and can produce a whole series of unexpected and hurtful outcomes. James' focus in verse 6, however, is not so much on the effect of speech on others but on the damage it can do to the speaker. Within the person exists a 'world of evil', says James, an evocative image which casts the tongue as a rival empire bent on our destruction. Bad talk can corrupt the whole person, says James, setting his or her entire existence 'on fire'. In this way, James reflects Jesus' teaching that a person is made 'unclean' not by what goes into the mouth but by what comes out of it:

> 17 Don't you see that whatever enters the mouth goes into the stomach and then out of the body? 18 But the things that come out of the mouth come from the heart, and these make a man 'unclean'. 19 For out of the heart come evil thoughts, murder, adultery, sexual immorality, theft, false testimony, slander. 20 These are what make a man 'unclean'; but eating with unwashed hands does not make him 'unclean'. (Matthew 15:17–20).

The forest fire set alight by the spark of the tongue has its origin in 'hell', says James (verse 6). The image is apt since hell, or *gehenna*, is associated with fire in the teaching of Jesus (Matthew 5:22; 18:9). Just as 'heaven' is frequently used as a circumlocution for God (Matthew 5:3; Luke 15:7; 15:18), it is possible 'hell' here refers to the devil himself. Corrupt speech, in other words, is satanic. This, of course, does not mean that the devil makes individuals say things they do not want to. By describing the ultimate origin of corrupt speech, James is really just stressing its true character. It is hellish and devilish. In 3:15 James will describe bitter envy and selfish ambition as similarly 'of the devil'.

As if this description were not enough, James turns the tongue into a kind of deadly snake in the fourth illustration (verses 7–8):

> [7] All kinds of animals, birds, reptiles and creatures of the sea are being tamed and have been tamed by man, [8] but no man can tame the tongue. It is a restless evil, full of deadly poison (James 3:7–8).

James lived in a culture that had tamed lions, elephants and even deadly vipers. The tongue, however, says the brother of Jesus, remains undomesticated—a completely wild and venomous creature. The phrase 'deadly poison' emphasises the tongue's power to harm *others*. The adjective 'restless' (*akatastatos*) means *unstable* and James has already used the term to describe the double-minded believer who is "unstable in all he does" (1:8). The noun form is used in 3:16 to describe the 'disorder' (*akatastasia*) which results from devilish wisdom. The point is, the tongue is a creature without stability and predictability. It is unruly because it has no foundation in God's order.

It probably goes without saying that James is employing hyperbole throughout these paragraphs. Following the style of Jesus (e.g. Matthew 5:29–30), James drives his point home about the dark potential of human words in absolute terms. We should not for a moment, however, think that James considers the taming of the tongue to be *impossible* or that human words *only ever* speak with venom. In verses 9– 12 James makes clear not only that the tongue can be used for good but also that believers are expected consistently to do so. This unruly creature is to find its rule and foundation in the purposes of God. As the introduction to the section makes clear, James fully expects believers to stop stumbling in what they say (3:2).

PRAISING AND CURSING; TREES AND THEIR FRUIT (3:9–12)

James 3:9–10 brings clarity and application to these provocative similes and metaphors:

> 9 With the tongue we praise our Lord and Father, and with it we curse men, who have been made in God's likeness.
> 10 Out of the same mouth come praise and cursing. My brothers, this should not be (3:9–10).

The 'speech' referred to throughout Chapter 3 has little to do with accidentally talking too much or putting your foot in your mouth; it is not even about swearing. These verses make clear that James is concerned with the incongruity of praising God on Sunday and speaking unkindly to human beings Monday through Saturday.

To 'praise' (*eulogeō*) is to declare the worthiness of someone. When directed towards God, as here, 'praise' usually refers to the declarations of God's people (sung and spoken) as they gather in public worship. This is how the word is used throughout the Book of Psalms, Israel's book of praises (Ps 26:12; 63:4–5; 68:26; 96:2; 103:20–23 and many others). Hence, James is probably referring here principally to the words we speak in honour of the Lord as we gather in church. We praise our 'Lord and Father', titles reminding us of the twin reasons for our thanksgiving to God: his mastery over us as his creatures and his grace toward us as his children. As throughout James, our submission to God's lordship is balanced with a reminder of God's fatherly compassion toward us.

To 'curse' is not to cast a spell or utter an expletive. It is to insult or denigrate another person with words. While the term may be used of a formulaic utterance intended to bring ill (Num 22:6), it frequently means little more than to denounce or revile: 'Do not revile the king even in your thoughts, or curse the rich in your bedroom, because a bird of the air may carry your words, and a bird on the wing may report what you say' (Eccl 10:20). We 'curse' whenever we speak *to* or *about* someone in a manner which disregards their status as those who 'have been made in God's likeness'

(3:9). One of the insights we gain as Christians is that men and women, though deeply flawed, are made in the image of God (Gen 1:26) and must be treated accordingly. To speak to others in a manner incongruous with this insight is to be untrue to one's own status as a member of God's people. As James says emphatically, though with some understatement: 'This should not be' (verse 10).

While it is true that Christians remain tarnished by sin in daily life, in the final two verses James stresses how unnatural it is that those who praise God would also curse their neighbours in whose image they are made:

> 11 Can both fresh water and salt water flow from the same spring? 12 My brothers, can a fig-tree bear olives, or a grapevine bear figs? Neither can a salt spring produce fresh water (3:11–12).

As mentioned earlier, James' use of these images resembles the teaching of Jesus on the subject of speech-ethics (Matthew 12:33–37). It also recalls the questions posed by Jesus in Matthew 7:16, 'Do people pick grapes from thornbushes, or figs from thistles?' In both cases, the answer is obvious. The reference to salt and fresh water springs may recall a saying of Jesus which did not find its way into the Gospels (another such statement is found in Acts 20:35). Alternatively, it may represent James' own expansion of the same theme. Either way, James and Jesus both insist that the quality of our lives is revealed by what we say.

The way we speak does not make us Christian, any more than the fruit determines the type of tree, but it does *disclose* what sort of people we are. It makes clear whether or not we are followers of the Messiah and of his royal law of love. In the logic of the letter of James, the word has been 'planted' in the believer (1:21); now the fruit of that word must be seen in the conduct of the believer. We are to speak to God with the praise due to him and to others with the honour due to them as creatures made in God's likeness. Put more simply, we are to love God and our neighbours with our words.

REFLECTIONS

1. Teachers today. 'Teachers' in James' day were effectively the preservers of the apostolic tradition. Without the teacher a congregation had limited access to the stories and teachings of Jesus and the testimonies of the first apostles. Of course, now that this material is codified in the writings of the New Testament, all Christians have immediate access to what was once mediated through teachers. The role of the teacher now, therefore, is that of an 'expounder' rather than 'preserver' of the apostolic tradition. The teacher is charged with helping the congregation see with clarity what the apostles said about Jesus and laid down for the churches. Whether through the professional 'sermon' or the more informal small group Bible study, teachers are a kind of window into 'the faith that was once for all entrusted to the saints' (Jude 3). Exaggerations, omissions and hobby horses are not permitted. All Christians must learn to control what comes out of the mouth but teachers must do so especially. For, as James insists, 'we who teach will be judged more strictly'.

2. Controlling the tongue. James describes our speaking as a kind of barometer of the whole of the ethical life: one who controls the tongue is able to keep the whole person in check. What we say and, just as importantly, how we say it is a fundamental expression of the royal law of love. This has implications for all of us: for the elderly church-goer who is constantly cranky with 'the teenagers of today'; for the zealous young believer who praises God in church but knocks his mates and snipes at his mum; for the business professional who addresses employees and shop assistants as inferiors; for the wife who knows just how to cut down her husband (without appearing to do so); for the preacher who is always admonishing the congregation rather than encouraging or praising them—as the apostles frequently did: e.g. Phil 4:1; 1 Thess 1:2–3; 3 John 2–4. The examples are endless, the point is the same: the tongue reveals the person just as the fruit reveals the tree.

3. *Men and women in the likeness of God.* James 3:9 reminds us of a motivation for Christian ethics that is sometimes neglected: the people around us have been made in the likeness of God. One might have thought that human beings have lost their status as creatures bearing God's likeness. The idea here is that what was granted at the creation (Gen 1:26) was lost through the fall. Men and women are now *only* sinners with little or no dignity as image bearers of the Creator. Hence, the motivation for Christian ethics is thought to derive entirely from grace: human beings deserve nothing but we should love them anyhow. James 3:9 follows Genesis 9:6 in insisting that (even after the fall) men and women share in the divine likeness/image and must treat one another in accordance with this high dignity. Grace is a fundamental motivation in Christian ethics but so is human dignity. The people we see around us—even the arrogant and unlovely—are creatures made in the likeness of our common Creator.

QUESTIONS FOR DISCUSSION

1. What things do you think a teacher might be judged 'more strictly' for? What might this stricter judgement look like? (Perhaps read 1 Corinthians 3:10–15 for further ideas).
2. Read Paul's account of teachers in 2 Timothy 2:1- 2. Imagine yourself back in time—to, say, the AD 30s- 50s—and describe the significance of 'teachers' before the New Testament was written. In what ways is the teacher's role today different and the same?
3. Read 3:3–5 again. Is James implying that the tongue actually controls our life? Why/why not? What exactly is the point of these similes?
4. Genesis 1:26, 9:6 and James 3:9 remind us that men and women bear the likeness of God. What are the implications of this for how we treat others?
5. Read Matthew 12:33–37. What similarities and differences can you see between Jesus' teaching and that of James 3:2–12?

8

Wisdom from Above; Life here Below

James 3:13–18

It is difficult to decide whether James 3:13–18 is a conclusion to the discussion of speech-ethics (3:1–12) or an introduction to the subject of 'fights and quarrels' (4:1–10). The resonances with both passages are strong. Perhaps it is best to view the passage as a 'pause' between Chapters 3 and 4 designed to remind readers of the central place of 'wisdom' in the Christian life.

Wisdom was one of the first themes discussed in the epistle. In the opening paragraph of the introduction James insisted: 'If any of you lacks wisdom, he should ask God, who gives generously to all without finding fault, and it will be given to him' (1:5). As previously stated, in keeping with the book of Proverbs and the teaching of Jesus, James views wisdom in *ethical* rather than intellectual terms. Wisdom involves an understanding of the shape of godliness in God's world.

Wisdom, you may recall, is also among the good and perfect gifts 'coming down from the Father' (1:17). In this way, wisdom and the 'word of truth' (1:18), one of the other gifts from above, are virtually indistinguishable. If we remember that for James the 'word of truth' is the tradition of Jesus, this synonymy is easily understood. Jesus himself was a teacher of wisdom and the very embodiment of wisdom itself (Matthew 11:19; 12:42; Mark 6:2; Luke 2:40). To embrace him, as we do when we embrace his gospel, is to embrace wisdom.

The above matrix of ideas should be held in mind as James calls on his readers to conform their lives to the way of Christ, to the wisdom which comes down from heaven:

> 13 Who is wise and understanding among you? Let him show it by his good life, by deeds done in the humility that comes from wisdom. 14 But if you harbour bitter envy and selfish ambition in your hearts, do not boast about it or deny the truth. 15 Such "wisdom" does not come down from heaven but is earthly, unspiritual, of the devil. 16 For where you have envy and selfish ambition, there you find disorder and every evil practice (3:13–16).

The section begins with a question which assumes its own answer: everyone would like to be known as 'wise and understanding'. Immediately, though, James challenges any who would claim to possess the wisdom of Christ. This wisdom will always be evident in 'deeds', a term which recalls the lengthy discussion of faith and deeds throughout Chapter 2.

Again, the logic of godly behaviour is clearly articulated in this passage. Performing good deeds does not make one wise, any more than fruit determines the species of tree. It is the other way around. Deeds 'come from wisdom', says James. They reveal whether or not a person is wise.

James stresses the importance of deeds done in the *humility* that comes from wisdom (verse 13). The word translated 'humility' is *prautēs* which means 'gentleness' or 'meekness'. The word has a special connection with the life and teaching of Jesus. In Matthew 11:29 Jesus and his 'yoke' (= teaching) are described in these terms:

> 28 Come to me, all you who are weary and burdened, and I will give you rest. 29 Take my yoke upon you and learn from me, for I am *gentle* and humble in heart, and you will find rest for your souls. 30 For my yoke is easy and my burden is light (Matthew 11:28–30).

The same terminology appears in Jesus' description of those who belong to God's kingdom ('Blessed are the *meek*, for they will inherit the earth' Matthew 5:5). Deeds of humility (or meekness), says James, prove our participation in the wisdom from heaven.

The opposite of deeds of humility are 'bitter envy' and 'selfish ambition' (verse 14). These are not necessarily internal states of mind—envying someone's house, for instance, or being ambitious for success. Both expressions speak of zeal to advance and dominate at the expense of others. These passions may arise from the 'heart' (verse 14) but they express themselves in relationships. The point is born out by verse 16 where James insists that envy and ambition lead to (community) 'disorder'.

Why would anyone 'boast' (verse 14) in their envy and ambition? It is possible that some in James' audience were so certain of their salvation through the confession of monotheism (2:18–19) that they exulted in their freedom from the ethical constraints of Jesus' teaching. More likely, however, is that James means that people who might have proudly answered the question of verse 13 ('Who is wise and understanding among you?') with 'I am!' ought to think again if their lives are marked by envy and ambition.

Such things, says James, are a 'denial' of the truth. The expression is literally 'to *lie* against the truth'. James means that to declare oneself wise when one's heart is full of envy and ambition is to speak falsely against God's truth. The 'truth' here, as elsewhere in James, is the traditions of Jesus, the 'word of truth' (1:18).

This false 'wisdom' comes not from heaven but from the earth—indeed, from the devil (verse 15). The mention of the devil here recalls the reference to 'hell' back in 3:6 (evil speech is 'set on fire by hell'). It also preempts the call in 4:7 to, 'Resist the devil'. It is important to observe that James perceives the devil's work in thoroughly ethical and relational terms: envy, selfish ambition (verse 14) and disorder (verse 16) are the evidence of the devil's work in a congregation.

James 3:17–18 describes what true wisdom involves, and the idea of 'deeds done in humility' is again close at hand:

> 17 But the wisdom that comes from heaven is first of all pure; then peace-loving, considerate, submissive, full of

> mercy and good fruit, impartial and sincere. [18] Peacemakers who sow in peace raise a harvest of righteousness.

The qualities listed here all have to do with relationships, i.e. with how we treat our neighbour. In English the word 'pure' often implies sexual innocence but this is not the primary connotation of the biblical term. The basic sense of the word pure (*agnos*) is *free from contamination*. In this context, it is a catch-all term for a life unpolluted by the qualities listed in verses 14–16. Such purity is basic to James' view of wisdom; hence, it is 'first of all'. The list of adjectives which follow are intended to fill out the meaning of 'pure' by describing the positive qualities that arise from wisdom.

'Peace-loving' has to do with *harmony* in our relationships; 'considerate' means giving *careful regard* to the needs and rights of others; 'submissive' refers to a willingness to *give in* to others, often a key to good relationships; 'full of mercy and good fruit' probably recalls the theme of *charity toward the poor* discussed in 2:13–16; 'impartial' is the *opposite of favouritism* (2:1); behind the word 'sincere' is the term *anupokritos* which literally translates as 'un-hypocritical', that is, not two-faced in relationships.

The final verse again highlights the relational emphasis of wisdom. Ultimately, James wants his readers to *make peace* amongst themselves (verse 18), that is, to end the fighting and discord hinted at in 3:16 and described in 4:1– 3, and foster harmonious friendships with one another. No doubt, James' teaching at this point is reliant upon that of Jesus: 'Blessed are the peacemakers, for they will be called sons of God' (Matthew 5:9).

Those who practice peace will reap a 'harvest of righteousness'. This final expression could refer to a harvest (literally, 'fruit') of righteous deeds here and now in the life of believers (2 Cor 9:10 and Heb 12:11). In this case, James would be saying that striving for peace in relationships will promote righteousness among God's people. Alternatively, the phrase might look forward to the final harvest in the kingdom of God (as in Gal 6:9). On this interpretation James would simply be saying that a commitment to peace here and now reaps rewards (for righteous behaviour) in God's kingdom. This would not refer to the reward of salvation as such but to the various other honours awaiting those who have been faithful, a theme discussed numerous times in the Scriptures (Matthew 6:4–6; 10:42; 1 Cor 3:14; Eph 6:8). Whichever interpretation of the 'harvest' one adopts, it is clear that James places a high premium on the responsibility of believers to be peacemakers, just as Jesus said.

James' call for wisdom, expressed in deeds of humility, sets up beautifully the call for deep repentance which follows in Chapter 4.

REFLECTIONS

1. Wisdom and relationships. The ethical and relational connotation of the word 'wisdom' reminds us again of something at the very core of our faith. Christianity is less about philosophical and theological insight ('wisdom' in a cognitive sense) and more about active relationships—with God and one another. Faithful Christian living involves *service* more than study, *love* more than contemplation and *harmony in relationships* more than personal equilibrium (a central goal of Buddhism). The question we must all ask in the light of James 3:13–18 is: Am I working for *peace* in my Christian community (and beyond)? If relationships are the field on which true wisdom is played out, there can be no greater test of the wise believer than his or her commitment to Christian harmony.

2. The devil and relationships. The mention of the 'devil' in 3:15 highlights something which will emerge elsewhere in James: whereas modern culture tends to highlight the 'mysterious' dimension of satanic activity (witchcraft, possession, etc.), James reminds us that fractured relationships are also, if not especially, devilish. We can see this in the narrative of Genesis 3. There, the devil undermines Eve's trust in God (Gen 3:2–5) which, in turn, damages the harmony between Adam and Eve themselves (3:12, 16). The same logic can be seen in a statement of the Apostle Paul, where discord in relationships falls straight into the devil's hands:

> 25 Therefore each of you must put off falsehood and speak truthfully to his neighbour, for we are all members of one body. 26 "In your anger do not sin": Do not let the sun go down while you are still angry, 27 and do not give the devil a foothold (Eph 4:25–27).

Just as we must not underestimate the satanic dangers of the occult, we must never miscalculate the devilish ploy to ruin Christian harmony.

QUESTIONS FOR DISCUSSION

1. How would you define 'wisdom' according to James 3:13–18? How does this compare with the contemporary use of the word?
2. Thinking of the aims of the devil read Genesis 3:2–16 and Ephesians 4:26–27. How do these verses compare/contrast with James' point in 3:14–15.
3. Read 3:16 again. What is the connection between 'envy and selfish ambition' and the rise of 'every evil practice'?
4. In 3:18 James says that those who practice peace will reap a 'harvest of righteousness'. What do you think this means? (Heb 12:11 and Gal 6:9 might help a little).

9

A Call to Repentance

James 4:1–12

James 4:1–12 is the central passage of the letter. Thus far, James has urged his readers to avoid favouritism (2:1–13), critcised them for ignoring the poor (2:14–26), warned them about the power of the tongue (3:1–12) and called on them to embrace wisdom (3:13–18). Now he pleads with his audience to repent. James 4:1–12 does not develop a new theme as such; it rather stops, and pleads with readers—ancient and modern—to take stock of the themes raised so far in the letter and make a decision about whether or not they will serve God and one another.

WAR, MURDER AND MONEY: THE PROBLEM (4:1–3)

The opening line is shocking in its description of what was going on in James' audience:

> 1 What causes fights and quarrels among you? Don't they come from your desires that battle within you? 2 You want something but don't get it. You kill and covet, but you cannot have what you want. You quarrel and fight. You do not have, because you do not ask God. 3 When you ask, you do not receive, because you ask with wrong motives, that you may spend what you get on your pleasures. (4:1–3)

The Greek of the opening sentence intensifies the drama of James' description. The expression 'fights and quarrels' is military language, literally 'wars and conflicts'. The reference to the desires 'that *battle* within you' uses another military term, the verb form of the word 'soldier'. Adding to this impression is James' accusation of 'murder': 'You kill and covet', he says—a reference to the sixth and tenth commandments (Ex 20:13, 17). He will throw the seventh commandment into the mix in verse 4 with his reference to 'adultery'.

What, we might ask, is going on here? Are we really to think that these first century Christians were engaged in some kind of murderous church war? Probably not. Similar to the teaching of 3:2–12 James is here using hyperbole and metaphor for dramatic effect. The use of the technical term for 'war' (*polemos*) in the opening line makes this immediately clear.

A further indication of the metaphorical nature of the language is found in the observation that, in early Christianity, acts of malice and hatred were often equated with 'murder'. It began with Jesus in his famous Sermon on the Mount:

> 21 You have heard that it was said to the people long ago, 'Do not murder, and anyone who murders will be subject to judgment.' 22 But I tell you that anyone who is angry with his brother will be subject to judgement (Matthew 5:21–22).

To be 'angry' or 'malicious' toward your neighbour, says Jesus, is akin to breaking the Sixth Commandment. The Apostle John, no doubt reflecting on Jesus' words, later said the same thing to his own congregations:

> 11 This is the message you heard from the beginning: We should love one another. 12 Do not be like Cain, who belonged to the evil one and murdered his brother ... 14 We know that we have passed from death to life, because we love our brothers. Anyone who does not love remains in death. 15 Anyone who hates his brother is a murderer, and you know that no murderer has eternal life in him. 16 This is how we know that love is: Jesus Christ laid down his life for us. And we ought to lay down our lives for our brothers. 17 If anyone has material possessions and sees his brother in need but has no pity on him, how can the love of God be in him? (1 John 3:11–17).

The matrix of ideas here is important to observe. To hate one's neighbours (that is, to refuse to love them) is to act like Cain, the first murderer in the Bible (Gen 4:3–8). Interestingly, the specific example offered by John for this love-hate polarity is the economic one. To refuse the needy is to hate them; to hate is to be a murderer.

A similar matrix of ideas is present in James 4:1–3. The 'murderous wars' going on amongst James' hearers are simply hateful acts, and these too have an economic dimension, as verses 2–3 make clear. The fights and quarrels in James' audience arise from *wanting something* but *not getting it* (verse 2). That 'something', of course, is *money* for which believers had been striving in order to 'spend what you get on your pleasures' (verse 3). The fractured relationships of which James speaks here—the 'wars and conflicts', the 'killing and coveting'—are the ones produced by a lust for wealth. Some in James' audience were so keen on economic advancement that they were willing to tread on others to achieve it. It all sounds disturbingly contemporary.

These believers were committing one of the most repugnant acts in the Bible: pursuing wealth at the expense of relationships. We already know from Chapter two that these believers were publicly favouring the rich and shaming the poor, and that they were refusing material assistance to the poor. James 3:3 puts all this in context: these believers were obsessed with accruing wealth to spend what they obtained on their pleasures. The word 'pleasure' here is *hēdonē* from which, of course, we get the word 'hedonism', that pursuit of life which regards 'pleasure' as the ultimate goal.

The words of verse 3 suggest, however, that it is permissible to pray to the Lord for financial assistance: 'When you ask, you do not receive, because you ask with wrong motives.' Jesus had encouraged his disciples to trust God for material support (Matthew 6:28–34) and to ask the Father for 'daily bread' (Matthew 6:11). A similar request for daily bread appears in Proverbs 30:8, 'Keep falsehood and lies far from me; give me neither poverty nor riches, but give me only my daily bread'. In both the teaching of

Jesus and the wisdom of Proverbs, the believer's prayer for material support is encouraged. But, as Proverbs 30:8 makes clear, the request must be moderate not selfish or extravagant. This is precisely the thought in James. The Father stands ready to support his needy children but his ear will be deaf to their requests if they are sullied by 'wrong motives'.

In the following verses James offers a profound assessment of this pursuit of wealth and pleasure.

FRIENDSHIP WITH THE WORLD: AN ASSESSMENT (4:4–6)

> 4 You adulterous people, don't you know that friendship with the world is hatred towards God? Anyone who chooses to be a friend of the world becomes an enemy of God. 5 Or do you think Scripture says without reason that the spirit he caused to live in us envies intensely? 6 But he gives us more grace. That is why Scripture says: "God opposes the proud but gives grace to the humble" (4:4–6).

There is much in the world that is beautiful, beneficial and pleasing to God, and there is a strong biblical tradition affirming this (Gen 1:31; 1 Tim 6:17). The Bible is equally clear in condemning any world-system which pursues wealth for pleasure at the expense of relationships. Choosing to befriend *that* 'world', says James, is an act of infidelity toward God: it turns us into an 'adulterous people' and an 'enemy of God'. The prophets of Israel likewise accused God's people of spiritual adultery (Jer 9:2; Ezek 6:9; Hos 1:2). James' readers will have felt the force of the allusion. The pursuit of wealth and pleasure at the expense of relationships is anathema to our Creator.

Verse 5 continues the theme of the betrayal of God. Here, however, we confront a couple of technical problems. Firstly, it is not clear which passage of 'Scripture' James refers to in verse 5, since nothing in our Old Testament uses the exact words quoted there. There are two possibilities. Either James had words in his Old Testament which are no longer in ours or, more likely, he is simply alluding to a scriptural theme rather than quoting a particular passage.

This leads to a second issue. Grammatically, there are several ways to translate the quotation/allusion in verse 5. The words in the body of the NIV text (quoted above) represent just one possible translation. The words in the NIV footnote are equally valid: 'God longs jealously for the spirit that he made to live in us.' This translation is preferable for two reasons: (a) The description of God as 'jealous' is the perfect counterpart to James' statement in the previous verse that God's people are 'adulterous', guilty of an illicit friendship with the world; (b) God's 'jealousy' over his wayward people is a very common theme in the Old Testament (e.g. Ex 20:5; Deut 32:16). James 4:5, as translated in the NIV footnote, would qualify as an allusion to many scriptural passages. The same cannot be said for the translation that appears in the body of the NIV text. James' point then in verse 5 is that God observes our adulterous love for the world (our craving for wealth over relationships) and he is jealous for our soul.

Verse 6 begins with 'but' (*de* in Greek). Despite God's jealousy over those who have befriended the world, 'he gives us more grace'. In other words, while God's jealousy might justly cause him to disown his adulterous wife, instead, he offers mercy. James quotes Proverbs 3:34 reminding readers that God opposes the proud (i.e. those who refuse James' message) and gives grace to the humble (i.e. those who accept the message). The words provide the perfect transition from James' damning assessment of his readers' current behaviour to his impassioned plea that they now return to God.

SUBMISSION TO GOD: A CALL TO REPENTANCE (4:7–10)

> 7 Submit yourselves, then, to God. Resist the devil, and he will flee from you. 8 Come near to God and he will come near to you. Wash your hands, you sinners, and purify your hearts, you double-minded. 9 Grieve, mourn and wail. Change your laughter to mourning and your joy to gloom. 10 Humble yourselves before the Lord, and he will lift you up (4:7–10).

On the one hand, the call to submit to God arises from the admonitions of the whole epistle so far. On the other hand, the 'then', or therefore (*oun*), at the beginning of verse 7 connects the sentence with what comes immediately before ('God ... gives grace to the humble' verse 6). In other words, the promise of 'grace', just as much as the exposure of sin, provides the rationale for this exhortation to repentance.

The leading sentence of this paragraph stands as a heading over the statements which follow. Submitting ourselves to God, then, is a multifaceted act. First, it involves resisting the devil, the *diabolos*, or 'diabolical one'. This relates to the world-system described in the previous paragraphs. God created the world for the enjoyment of *relationships*—the true currency of creation. To flirt with a world-system which perverts this intention—one that pursues wealth and pleasure at the *expense* of relationships—is to offer allegiance to the diabolical one. As stated in connection with James 3:15, the church must remember that the devil is seen not only in the occult but also, and perhaps especially, in a lifestyle that values the dollar more than our neighbour. Resist the devil, says James, 'and he will flee'.

The word 'resist' (*anthistēmi*) comes from the root *to stand*. It means to make a stand against something or someone. James is not so much talking about resisting temptations; he is calling for a new resolve to live in opposition to the ways of Satan. The Apostle Paul uses the same language in a similar context:

> Therefore put on the full armour of God, so that when the day of evil comes, you may be able to stand your ground (*anthistēmi*), and after you have done everything, to stand (*histēmi*) (Eph 6:13).

Secondly, submission to God involves 'coming near to God'. Throughout Scripture this expression is sometimes associated with the priests who, in their temple activities, are said to draw near to God (Ex 19:22; Ez 40:46; 45:4; Heb 10:1). The concept is also occasionally broadened to include the spiritual renewal of all God's people (Zeph 3:2 and Heb 10:22 where the drawing near of the priests in 10:1 is said to be possible for all believers in the new covenant). This is the sense in James 4:8. The change required by James is not a mere socialist rejection of the habits of the rich; it is a personal move toward the Creator, allowing his influence to permeate our lives. The Book of James is not simply about morality; it is about devotion to our God expressed in devotion to our neighbour. The promise for those who draw near to God is that God will draw near to them, an expression reminiscent of the call to repentance in Malachi 3:7, 'Return to me, and I will return to you'.

Thirdly, true submission to God involves the admission of and purification from sins: 'Wash your hands, you sinners, and purify your hearts, you double-minded' (verse 8). Throughout the Bible, the term 'sinner' is used of those who walk in rebellion towards God, typically in contrast to the 'righteous' who walk in right relationship with God (see Ps 1:5; 37:37–38; Prov 11:31; 13:6; Eccl 2:26; 7:26; Isa 1:27–28; Luke 15:7; 1 Pet 4:18). The 'righteous', of course, continue to sin, but when they do they readily repent and seek God's forgiveness. Their lives are not characterised by resistance to God's ways and so they are not 'sinners' in the typical scriptural sense of the word. Given this biblical background, James' use of the term 'sinners' in verse 8 will have been shocking to his first hearers. He is not accusing them of the failings common to all believers this side of the Kingdom (the sense in which we are all 'sinners'); he is declaring them to be in a state of rebellion against the ways of God. Their murderous craving after wealth places them in direct enmity with the Lord. They are 'double-minded', furthermore, an expression which refers to one's split loyalties (as in 1:8)—to God and to the world. James' hearers are Christians in name and sinners in action.

But sinners can be forgiven, and the terms 'washing' and 'purifying' (verse 8) are traditional Jewish words for the repentance that leads to God's mercy. In Exodus 30:19–21 hand washing is required of Aaron and his sons prior to entering the Tent of Meeting, the place of God's presence. The action is symbolic of the removal of ritual and moral impurity which keeps one from the holy God. While James has no cultic context in mind, he borrows this cultic image to evoke a similar notion of cleansing. The thought is similar to that in Isaiah 1:16, 'wash and make yourselves clean. Take your evil deeds out of my sight! Stop doing wrong'. The term 'purify' also comes from Old Testament cultic language (e.g. Num 8:21) but is used in an ethical context in the New Testament (1 Pet 1:22; 1 John 3:3).

Fourthly, and finally, when a sinner submits to God it will involve a godly sorrow: 'Grieve, mourn and wail. Change your laughter to mourning and your joy to gloom' (verse 9). James is no doubt recalling his brother's words: 'Blessed are you who weep now, for you will laugh ... Woe to you who laugh now, for you will mourn and weep' (Luke 6:21–25). Those who pursue wealth at the expense of relationships may at times 'laugh' in moments of fleeting pleasure, but great sadness awaits them, said Jesus. Reflecting on this, James begs his readers to exchange the 'laughter' of the world for a deep and sorrowful repentance.

It is in the context of sorrowful repentance that James offers the wonderful promise of verse 10: 'Humble yourselves before the Lord, and he will lift you up.' The words, of course, recall the quotation from Proverbs 3:34 back in verse 6, 'God ... gives grace to the humble'. Those who submit to God, who humble themselves before him, will be granted a high place in God's eyes: they will be lifted up. Since 'to humble' oneself literally means to *lower* oneself, the language of 'lifting' is intended as a resolution. Those who bow down before the great King prostrating their lives before him in sorrowful repentance will be raised up to stand tall and forgiven in his presence.

James' words resonate with the teaching of Jesus who, in the parable of the Pharisee and Tax-collector, insisted that humble, mournful confession of sin was the path way to exaltation:

> [13] "But the tax collector stood at a distance. He would not even look up to heaven, but beat his breast and said, 'God, have mercy on me, a sinner.' [14] "I tell you that this man, rather than the other (the Pharisee), went home justified before God. For everyone who exalts himself will be humbled, and he who humbles himself will be exalted" (Luke 18:13–14).

This is precisely the idea behind James' words in Chapter 4. Yes, his readers had pursued wealth at the expense of relationships. In the language of James they had started wars, committed murder and developed an adulterous friendship with the world. But God stands ready, insists James, to cleanse the impure, to forgive the sinner, to lift up the humble. For all the warnings and commands of the Book of James, ultimately this is an epistle of grace.

NO LONGER JUDGING: AN EPILOGUE (4:11–12)

James 4:11–12 is like an epilogue to the call to repentance in 4:1–10. If verses 7–10 emphasise the God-ward nature of repentance, verses 11–12 bear out some of its human-ward implications:

> [11] Brothers, do not slander one another. Anyone who speaks against his brother or judges him speaks against the law and judges it. When you judge the law, you are not keeping it, but sitting in judgment on it. [12] There is only one Lawgiver and Judge, the one who is able to save and destroy. But you—who are you to judge your neighbour? (4:11–12).

While the references to 'fights and quarrels' (4:1) would certainly include the 'slandering' and 'judging' mentioned here in 4:11–12, James obviously believed these latter themes deserved individual attention here at the conclusion to his call to repentance.

There is a near synonymy between the words 'slander', 'speak against' and 'judge'. All of them refer to denigrating one's neighbour publicly. To *judge* is to go beyond simply discerning people or things; it is to write them off and condemn them and, in this case, to do so openly.

To judge other people, says James, is to judge the 'law' itself. The law referred to here could be Jesus' command, 'Do not judge, or you too will be judged' (Matthew 7:1). However, it is more likely to be a reference to the royal law mentioned in James 2:8 ('Love your neighbour as yourself') which, as previously stated, comes from Leviticus 19:18 and was brought into the centre of the ethical life by Jesus (Matthew 22:39–40). To condemn one's brother is clearly to disregard the command to love. It is therefore to sit in judgment of the royal law, to lift oneself above what Jesus had declared.

James' reference to there being 'only one Lawgiver and Judge' underlines the absurdity of a mere mortal judging the law by condemning his neighbour. Presumably, the lawgiver and judge is God himself (Isa 33:22) who alone has the power to save and destroy (cf. Matthew 10:28). It is possible, though, that James also has in mind the Messiah as the agent of God's law, salvation and judgment (Matthew 25:31–33; Acts 17:31; Rom 2:16). In 5:8–9 James will apply the title 'Judge' to the returning Lord Jesus. Either way, in light of God's (and the Messiah's) sole prerogative to judge humanity, the obvious question is the one James asks (rhetorically) at the conclusion of the discussion: 'But you—who are you to judge your neighbour?' (4:12). No answer is expected because no answer can be given.

REFLECTIONS

1. Greed as adultery and idolatry. In describing the pursuit of wealth (at the expense of relationships) as spiritual 'adultery' (verse 4) James strikes a theme that resounds elsewhere throughout the New Testament: riches are sometimes a rival 'god' seducing God's people away from their proper worship. The theme appears in a well-known statement of Jesus:

> No-one can serve two masters. Either he will hate the one and love the other, or he will be devoted to the one and despise the other. You cannot serve both God and Money (Matthew 6:24).

A similar idea is found in the Apostle Paul's statement that 'greed is idolatry' (Col 3:5). In other words, to pursue wealth is to worship another god. In the language of James it is to commit adultery with another lover.

Wealth *per se* is not the problem. It is a chasing after wealth 'to spend what you get on you pleasures' (4:3) that amounts to spiritual adultery and idolatry. Amassing money in order to dress in great clothes, eat at fine restaurants, holiday in beautiful locations and fill the home with all the modern comforts: this, says James, is a betrayal of our Creator. Why? Because God has granted us the gifts of his creation not for individual pleasure but for the enhancement of human relationships, which is the true currency of life. Not using our provisions for their intended purpose is a rejection of the Provider himself. Of course, the rich are not expected to become poor themselves. But they are expected to be 'rich in good deeds, and to be generous and willing to share' (1 Tim 6:18). That is, they are to use their wealth relationally.

2. Gaining good judgment. When the Bible warns against *judging* others (as in James 4:11–12) it is not forbidding the formation of critical opinions about certain actions, ideas or people. This point needs to be underlined in the modern context. In some quarters of the church the scriptural commands against judging are used to justify the willing acceptance of ideas and practices the Bible actually condemns. It is noteworthy that the passage most often used to support this view makes clear that 'not judging' does not mean 'not discerning something to be wrong'. The words 'Do not judge' (Matthew 7:1) are quickly followed up with a call for critical discernment:

> [5] ... first take the plank out of your own eye, and then you will see clearly to remove the speck from your brother's eye. [6] Do not give dogs what is sacred; do not throw your pearls to pigs (Matthew 7:5–6).

The reality is, the Scriptures regularly urge us to assess the validity of certain teachings and practices (Matthew 7:15; 7:20; Mark 8:15; Luke 12:57; Acts 15:19; Rom 16:17; 1 Cor 6:5; Phil 3:2). This kind of judgment is an important feature of faithful discipleship. The 'judging' condemned in the Bible is the type that seeks to decry people and write them off.

QUESTIONS FOR DISCUSSION

1. Reread 4:1–3. How do you think the pursuit of wealth could have caused such problems in the church?
2. Why do you think the Bible associates 'discord' and 'hatred' with 'murder' (James 4:1–3; 1 John 3:11–17)?
3. In what way could 4:7–10 be described as the central paragraph of the letter?
4. Based on this passage, what place does grace have in James' thinking?
5. Given that James has already offered a lengthy treatment of the subject of the tongue (3:1–12), why do you think he returns to the theme here in 4:11–12 after his call to repentance (4:7–10)?

10

Warnings and Promises

James 4:13–5:11

Despite the new chapter commencing at 5:1 and the 'ever-present' subheadings of modern Bibles (at 4:13; 5:1 and 5:7), James 4:13–5:11 is actually one self-contained section. It is a three point sermonette within the letter. The first two sections are joined together by the recurring introductory phrase 'Now listen, you ...' (4:13; 5:1). The third section is linked to the second by the conjunction 'therefore' (*oun*), translated here simply as 'then': 'Be patient, *then*, brothers, until the Lord's coming' (5:7). The 'then' (or 'therefore') makes clear that the encouragement to be patient arises out of what has just been said in the previous section.

With this three-fold structure in mind, 4:13 - 5:11 can be seen to speak directly to three different audiences within ancient society. The first are the 'merchants' (4:13–17), the upwardly mobile of antiquity, those who had the means and ambition to travel abroad and make money. The second group are the rich (5:1–6) and, in particular, the wealthy land owners who employed people by the thousands and who, without any industrial relations legislation in the ancient world, frequently mistreated their labourers. The third group are what you might call the faithful oppressed (5:7–11), that is, Christians who belonged to the great mass of the working and slave classes and whose lives were often made hell by the actions of the rich and powerful.

THE ARROGANT MERCHANTS (4:13–17)

We begin with the merchants. James identifies them in the stereotypical words of verse 13:

> Now listen, you who say, "Today or tomorrow we will go to this or that city, spend a year there, carry on business and make money" (4:13).

No one in antiquity will have missed the relevance of these words. In a period of massive imperial expansion and increasingly easy travel (made possible by the famous Roman roads), the vast wealth of the Roman empire began to trickle down the social ladder and into the broader economy. The result was that, in the first century AD, materialism, decadence and financial corruption had become rife. Lucan, the Roman rhetorician and poet (and James' contemporary), wrote of Roman wealth: 'Fortune introduced excess of wealth, and morals collapsed before prosperity; the spoils of war encouraged extravagance ... public office was stolen through bribery' (Lucan 1.160ff). At about the time James wrote his epistle, millions of denarii a year (a denarius was a day's wages) was being spent by wealthy citisens on luxuries from India, China and Arabia—spices, jewelry, silk, perfume and so on. It is in this climate that Jesus' words will have struck his audience as particularly relevant:

> So do not worry, saying, 'What shall we eat?' or 'What shall we drink?' or 'What shall we wear?' For *the pagans run after all these things* (Matt 6:31–32).

Merchants, of course, had been around for millennia but with the surge in available wealth in the first century the international opportunities for such traders were greatly increased. First century merchants were as eager for their *denarius* as anything we observe today. Against this backdrop James' words in 4:13 will have had special resonance.

There is, of course, nothing wrong with the entrepreneurial spirit: the famous woman of Proverbs 31 is praised for her business sense:

> She selects wool and flax and works with eager hands ... She considers a field and buys it; out of her earnings she plants a vineyard ... She makes linen garments and sells them, and supplies the merchants with sashes (Prov 31:13–24).

The problem is: merchants, particularly successful ones, were prone to arrogance. They were moving up the social scale waving smugly at those they passed. You can almost hear them at the local market-places and the banquets: 'Oh, yes, I have a shipment of spices arriving tomorrow from Egypt. I'll be taking them down to Ephesus on Tuesday before heading to Rome for trade negotiations with some well-to-do households.' To all this James responds in his typical aphoristic, Jesus-like style:

> Why, you do not even know what will happen tomorrow. What is your life? You are a mist that appears for a little while and then vanishes (4:14).

James is right. The precious stock could be shipwrecked on the way from Egypt, the merchandise could be raided on the way to Ephesus, the households of Rome could find a cheaper price from another merchant. Moreover, our lives—even successful ones—are simply 'mist' appearing and disappearing without a trace. Here James recalls the theme struck in the introduction to his letter: 'the rich man will fade away even while he goes about his business.' (1:11).

James then insists that merchants—indeed, all of us—should think and act as those who live under the rule of God not the reign for money:

> 15 Instead, you ought to say, "If it is the Lord's will, we will live and do this or that." 16 As it is, you boast and brag. All such boasting is evil. 17 Anyone, then, who knows the good he ought to do and doesn't do it, sins (4:15–17).

It is important to note that James does not reject forward-planning outright. One may still validly prepare to 'live' and do 'this or that'. James' point is simply that such planning should always be done under the banner: 'if the Lord wills'. Otherwise, it is a life characterised by 'boasting' and 'bragging'. These terms are near synonyms highlighting the presumption of the merchants to think that they control anything, let alone their travels, material security and life.

The recommendation that people acknowledge the supremacy of God's will in the affairs of life is not unique to the Judeo-Christian tradition. The pagan philosopher Epictetus writing just a few decades after James speaks of a sailor's dependence on the winds and on God's will:

> For God has not made you steward of the winds, but Aeolus [the divine ruler of the winds]. 'What then?' We must make the best of what is under our control, and take the rest as its nature is. 'How, then, is its nature?' As God wills (Epictetus, *Discourses* 1.1.17).

The difference, of course, between Epictetus and James is that James knew it is the one true God (with his Messiah) who rules heaven and earth, and it is to him we must surrender our ambitions. Did James expect his hearers literally to implement the motto 'If it is the Lord's will' into their daily affairs? If he did, it is likely he intended it not as a legalistic requirement or superstitious habit but as a healthy foil to the boasting that was already on the lips of some (4:13).

James underlines the importance of living by this motto in the final words of the section: 'Anyone, then, who knows the good he ought to do and doesn't do it, sins' (4:17). The sudden change from the second person ('*you* boast and brag') to the third person ('*anyone* who') may suggest that James is quoting a well known proverb. The saying certainly sounds proverbial and its grammar is considered Semitic, leading some to suggest it is a saying of Jesus. Whatever the origin—and James may well have coined it himself—James' point is that Christian merchants who refuse to acknowledge that they live and breathe and work by God's will are engaging in sin. They have departed from the path of Christ.

THE RICH OPPRESSORS (5:1–6)

James' warnings to merchants give him cause in the next section to speak of those one step up the social 'food chain'.

In 5:1–6 James denounces the rich or, more accurately, the corrupt rich:

> [1] Now listen, you rich people, weep and wail because of the misery that is coming upon you. [2] Your wealth has rotted, and moths have eaten your clothes. [3] Your gold and silver are corroded. Their corrosion will testify against you and eat your flesh like fire. You have hoarded wealth in the last days. [4] Look! The wages you failed to pay the workmen who mowed your fields are crying out against you. The cries of the harvesters have reached the ears of the Lord Almighty. [5] You have lived on earth in luxury and self-indulgence. You have fattened yourselves in the day of slaughter. [6] You have condemned and murdered innocent men, who were not opposing you (5:1–6).

The words 'Now listen, you' recall the same expression addressed to merchants in 4:13 indicating that what we have here, as previously noted, is part two of a threefold unit.

James has used strong language in the letter before but these words take his caustic tone to a new level. Here, he appears to be consigning the rich to hell without possibility of repentance and mercy. The question is: to whom does he direct these words, and why?

It is essential to recognise that James' style in this paragraph has much in common with a Jewish literary form known as the *prophetic lament*. Readers of modern media know full well how to interpret the various genres present in, say, our newspapers. We do not need a style-guide in order to recognise and interpret the editorial, the letters section, the cartoons, a satirical piece or the TV guide. The societies of biblical times had their own genres and the Bible itself contains examples of most of them: history, poetry, parable, aphorism, hymn, apocalyptic and epistle. One such ancient genre was the prophetic lament. Here, the prophet denounces an oppressor *not* as a warning to the one addressed but as a comfort to the oppressed (who overhear the denunciation). Hence, in the prophetic lament there is no expectation that the evildoer will hear the message—that is almost irrelevant. The words are intended for the benefit of those suffering under the tyrant. They are a vivid rhetorical way of saying to the faithful, 'Hang in there: help is on the way; the tyrant will soon be overthrown'.

To offer some examples: as part of his message of judgement and comfort to Israel, the prophet Ezekiel turns for, several chapters, to denounce the oppressive regimes around Israel. One of them is Egypt:

> 1 ... the word of the LORD came to me: 2 "Son of man, set your face against Pharaoh king of Egypt and prophesy against him and against all Egypt. 3 Speak to him and say: 'This is what the Sovereign LORD says: "'I am against you, Pharaoh king of Egypt, you great monster lying among your streams. You say, "The Nile is mine; I made it for myself." 4 But I will put hooks in your jaws and make the fish of your streams stick to your scales (Ez 29:1–4).

Pharaoh and the Egyptians almost certainly never heard the words of Ezekiel, who was a Judean exile in Babylon. That is beside the point. The lament is intended for the prophet's true audience, the people of God who had long known the tyranny of Egypt.

The second example comes from Jesus who, in the middle of his instructions to the seventy-two missionaries, denounced certain towns of Galilee in similar prophetic fashion:

> 13 "Woe to you, Korazin! Woe to you, Bethsaida! For if the miracles that were performed in you had been performed in Tyre and Sidon, they would have repented long ago, sitting in sackcloth and ashes. 14 But it will be more bearable for Tyre and Sidon at the judgment than for you. 15 And you, Capernaum, will you be lifted up to the skies? No, you will go down to the depths (Luke 10:13–15).

Clearly, all three towns were not within earshot of these words. The lament is intended not for the towns themselves but for Jesus' disciples who will know rejection and persecution from towns such as these. The denunciation is intended as a promise to the disciples that those who oppose God (and his Messiah) will find themselves overthrown.

James 5:1–6 functions in a similar manner: it is a classic prophetic lament. It is designed not as a warning to rich oppressors within the church (of which there were probably none) but as a comfort to the oppressed themselves (of which there were probably quite a few). The theme of divine judgment, then, as so often in the Bible, functions in this passage as a pledge to the wounded that God knows their pain and will one day bring the healing of his powerful justice. Wrongs will be righted; fortunes will be reversed.

The rich are to 'weep and wail' (verse 1), words reminiscent of the call to repentance in 4:9. The difference here, though, is that the sorrow is not that of remorse over sin; rather, it is the grief of the terror of judgement which awaits, described here as the 'misery that is coming upon you'. The use of the present tense, 'coming upon', heightens the warning. Judgement is not some vague future event; it is already on the move. This vivid description of judgement intensifies in verses 2–3 where James switches to the perfect tense. The wrath of God toward the rich is so sure that it can be said to have already occurred: 'Your wealth has rotted, and moths have eaten your clothes. Your gold and silver are corroded.'

The crimes of the 'rich' are listed through verses 3–6. Not only have they hoarded wealth (verse 3) and lived in luxury and indulgence (verse 5), they have done so at the expense of the poor, withholding wages from the field workers (verse 4), people who literally lived on the previous day's earnings. The reference in verse 6 to 'condemning' and 'murdering' innocent men could be hyperbole (as in 4:1–2). However, given that day-laborers often worked literally for their 'daily bread', the language may well be realistic. The word 'condemn' may also have legal overtones recalling one of James' previous indictments against the rich ('dragging you into court' 2:6).

Injustice of this kind does not go unnoticed. The cries of the oppressed have reached heaven (verse 4). This picture of the earthly pleas of the oppressed reaching the ears of

God comes from the Old Testament (Gen 4:10; Ex 2:23) as does the warning about withholding rights or wages from poor workers (Lev 19:13; Deut 24:14–15; Jer 22:13; Mal 3:5). The one who hears the complaints of the defrauded is the 'Lord Almighty'. The word translated 'Almighty' is actually a Greek transliteration of the Hebrew word *Sabaōth* which means 'hosts/armies'. The Defender of the poor is none other than the Lord of the heavenly warriors. The same expression appears in a similar context in Isaiah:

> Woe to you who add house to house and join field to field till no space is left and you live alone in the land. The *LORD Almighty* has declared in my hearing: "Surely the great houses will become desolate, the fine mansions left without occupants (Isa 5:8–9).

And, so, James advises the rich to prepare for the worst. Their indulgent lifestyle has done little more than fatten them up for the 'day of slaughter', a phrase from the Old Testament (Isa 30:25; Jer 12:3) which describes the final, unstoppable moment of divine wrath against the evil of the world.

This striking passage is written to reassure the oppressed that a day of justice awaits the world. It is in this context that the early Christians cried, 'How long, Sovereign Lord' (Rev 6:10) and *Maranatha* ('Come, O Lord' 1 Cor 16:22). Judgment for ancient believers was not a cause of embarrassment; it was a source of comfort and longing as they awaited the righting of the wrongs of the world.

While not its primary purpose, this passage may also be read as a subtle warning to any believer who would dare to participate in the oppression of the poor.

THE FAITHFUL OPPRESSED (5:7–11)

In 5:7–11 James shifts from a prophetic lament about rich oppressors to a word of consolation to the faithful oppressed:

> 7 Be patient, then, brothers, until the Lord's coming. See how the farmer waits for the land to yield its valuable crop and how patient he is for the autumn and spring

> rains. [8] You too, be patient and stand firm, because the Lord's coming is near. (5:7–8)

As stated previously, the 'then' or 'therefore' in verse 7 makes clear that the call to be patient arises from a knowledge of the fate of the world's oppressors. James addresses his readers not in the rather impersonal 'Now listen, you' (4:13; 5:1) but with the more affectionate 'brothers'. James urges his suffering brethren not to rise up in rebellion against those who oppose and oppress them, but to await God's day of justice as a farmer awaits the seasons.

The word translated (the Lord's) 'coming' in verse 7 and verse 8 employs the important Greek term, *parousia*, which often refers to an *eminent appearance*. The term was commonly used of an official appearance of the king or emperor in one of his cities. The expression 'the *parousia* of the Lord', then, casts Jesus as the true emperor of the world soon to make an official appearance on behalf of his oppressed people. On that day, the Messiah will exact the judgement on oppressors described in 5:1–6. This will be nothing other than the fulfillment of a key messianic text of the Old Testament:

> A shoot will come up from the stump of Jesse; from his roots a Branch will bear fruit. [2] The Spirit of the LORD will rest on him—the Spirit of wisdom and of understanding, the Spirit of counsel and of power, the Spirit of knowledge and of the fear of the LORD—[3] and he will delight in the fear of the LORD. He will not judge by what he sees with his eyes, or decide by what he hears with his ears; [4] but with righteousness he will judge the needy, with justice he will give decisions for the poor of the earth. He will strike the earth with the rod of his mouth; with the breath of his lips he will slay the wicked (Isa 11:1–4).

In light of the messianic *parousia* believers are to 'stand firm' or literally 'strengthen your hearts'. This is a reference to remaining solid in one's resolve to walk according to the teaching of Christ—not craving the power and wealth of the oppressors but living in anticipation of the 'Lord's coming'.

Part of being strong in the way of Christ is a decision to put an end to the infighting going on among some in James' audience:

> Don't grumble against each other, brothers, or you will be judged. The Judge is standing at the door! (5:9).

The word 'grumble' here does not simply refer to the odd complaint or whinging. The word is emotionally charged, often meaning something like 'groaning', and James is probably alluding euphemistically to the serious quarrels discussed earlier in the letter (4:1–3). This is groaning/grumbling 'against each other'.

The reason for ending such disputes is that the 'Judge' is 'standing at the door' (5:9), that is, about to commence his judgment. Here the Judge is the soon-to-appear Messiah (cf. 4:12 where the Judge is God himself) and the phrase 'standing at the door' comes straight out of Jesus' teaching about his own role on the Day of Judgment (Mark 13:26–29; Luke 13:23–27).

The 'Christology' of 5:9 (i.e. its estimation of Christ's status) is very *high*. Jesus is not merely the teacher whose wisdom sets the criteria of judgment; he is the instrument of divine judgment itself. Giving Jesus the title 'Judge' is all the more significant in view of the statement just a few paragraphs earlier (4:12) that there is 'only one Judge' (i.e. God). While James probably did not intend to imply Jesus' full divinity (a doctrine taught elsewhere in the New Testament), he does cast Jesus as the personification of one of the biblical God's central qualities (and activities): his justice.

James' main point in this section, however, is not to admonish his hearers with news of judgment but to encourage them with the promise of deliverance. A tone of comfort immediately returns to the remaining verses of the section:

> 10 Brothers, as an example of patience in the face of suffering, take the prophets who spoke in the name of the Lord. 11 As you know, we consider blessed those who have persevered. You have heard of Job's perseverance and

> have seen what the Lord finally brought about. The Lord is full of compassion and mercy (5:10–11).

James here resumes the theme of patient endurance in the face of suffering (presumably at the hands of the rich oppressors). He wants his readers to learn from the example of the ancient prophets, many of whom experienced terrible persecution (1 Kings 19:1; Neh 9:26). In the famous Beatitudes ('blessings') Jesus too urged his disciples to look to the prophets as examples of endurance in the face of persecution:

> 11 "Blessed are you when people insult you, persecute you and falsely say all kinds of evil against you because of me.
> 12 Rejoice and be glad, because great is your reward in heaven, for in the same way they persecuted the prophets who were before you (Matthew 5:11–12).

That James has this particular saying of Jesus in mind is made likely by verse 11: 'As you know, we consider blessed those who have persevered.' In other words, it is a well known Christian practice, says James, that those who persevere like the prophets are to be called 'blessed'. The word's of Jesus recorded in Matthew 5:11–12 must lie behind this early Christian habit.

One such blessed individual of the past was Job (verse 11). His story of endurance and vindication serves, says James, as a model of what it means to look forward to 'what the Lord will finally bring about'. In Job's case, God restored his health and wealth (Job 42:12–17). In the case of believers, the Lord will do much, much more.

The basis of this future hope is, of course, God's very character. And so James concludes with words reminiscent of Psalm 103:8, 'The Lord is full of compassion and mercy' (5:11). These words are not so much a reference to God's desire to save sinners (as true as that is); they are a reminder that the judgement to come is as much a display of divine compassion as it is of wrath. When God overthrows the tyrannies of the world, the depth of his love for the faithful oppressed will be plain for all to see.

REFLECTIONS

1. Keeping aspirations in check. James' words to merchants provide a salient reminder to many in modern Western societies. Merchants were the 'aspirational' class of antiquity, those who longed for more wealth and made plans to achieve it. Aspiration for wealth appears to be the default outlook today. Employers urge us to climb the 'company' ladder (often simply to extract our productivity). Advertisers constantly bombard us with the comforts we *really need.* And our own hearts cry out for just a little more status, just a little more travel and just a little more money.

While such aspirations may not in themselves be wrong, they are frequently accompanied by an arrogance that is. James urges us to take stock of our lives and humbly acknowledge two things. Firstly, our lives are a 'mist'. At times, I think I am quite accomplished; some days I even think I am actually quite important. The reality is: I am a frail and fleeting creature in God's universe and, although I am loved and treasured by the Creator, my life will soon be gone and forgotten—I am a mist, says the Lord's brother. Secondly, and relatedly, amid my ambitions in this world I must live under the banner: 'if it is the Lord's will.' All of my sleeping, waking, earning and breathing come from God's hand. James' point is that we should think, act and talk like we know that.

2. Judgment as compassionate justice. James 5:1–11 reminds us of a very important biblical emphasis. At its core, the theme of God's judgement is not simply a theological scare-tactic designed to make the non-religious more religious. Judgement is the pledge of the loving God to oppressed humanity that he hears their cry for justice and will one day bring his justice to bear on every act of tyranny.

There is no question the Bible speaks of judgement in other contexts as well. For instance, biblical writers frequently warn hypocritical believers that they may well find themselves numbered among the tyrannous when God's judgment comes (1 Sam 15:22–23; Ps 50:1–23;

Isa 1:10–20; 66:1–4; Luke 12:47–48; Luke 20:46–47). But this should not obscure the fact that the theme of God's judgement is a promise from a loving Creator that he will one day reverse the fortunes of the poor and oppressed and bring justice to the world (Ex 2:23; 22:21–24; Isa 10:1–3; 11:1–4; Jer 2:31–37; Ez 22:27–31; Amos 5:1–27; Zech 7:8–14; Matthew 25:31–46; Rev 18:19–24). The Day of Judgment, therefore, is a wonderful day. It is God's day of justice.

QUESTIONS FOR DISCUSSION

1. What do you see as the logical connection between the three sections (4:13–17, 5:1–6 and 5:7–11)?
2. Read the account of the merchant-like woman in Proverbs 31:10–31. What distinguishes her from the figure warned in James 4:13–17?
3. In your own words what is the purpose of James 5:1–6 within the epistle as a whole?
4. What is the basis of Christian patience in 5:7–11?

11

Telling the Truth

James 5:12

How does James 5:12 relate to what comes before it and/or after it? The theme of judgment at the end of the verse may provide a link back to the previous paragraphs (verses 1–11). Alternatively (or in addition), the topic of *speaking* (the truth) may introduce what follows about praying and singing (verses 13–14). However, these connections are subtle and are unlikely to have been picked up by those who first heard the letter (remember, most of the New Testament epistles were composed for public reading not private analysis). Also the introductory phrase 'above all' sets it apart from what precedes and suggests a new topic. James 5:12 appears, then, to be a lone instruction which James felt necessary to include for his hearers before the close of the letter:

> Above all, my brothers, do not swear—not by heaven or by earth or by anything else. Let your "Yes" be yes, and your "No", no, or you will be condemned (5:12).

'Above all' does not mean that this verse is the most important in the letter. This is a customary phrase designed to bring emphasis to a statement (1 Pet 4:8; 2 Pet 1:20). It is a way of saying 'Let me underline this!' Perhaps James added this emphasis in order to counterbalance the impression left by treating the topic so briefly. This may be a brief word but it is an important one.

James 5:12 contains the epistle's most obvious allusion to a specific statement of Jesus. As with the other allusions, however, James feels no need to present the words as a quotation. James' hearers were well acquainted with the words of their Messiah—their 'teachers' were charged with making sure of this. As I said earlier, for the first Christians the Jesus-tradition constituted the 'word of truth' (1:18) and the 'perfect law that gives freedom' (1:25). It was already at the centre of the church's life and public worship long before James wrote this letter. Hence, unlike in a modern commentary no explicit cross-referencing to Jesus' teaching was needed for James' audience. The faintest hint of something the Messiah said recalled for ancient believers the very words of life.

Let me recall for us the portion of the Jesus-tradition James has in mind here in 5:12:

> 33 Again, you have heard that it was said to the people long ago, 'Do not break your oath, but keep the oaths you have made to the Lord.' 34 But I tell you, Do not swear at all: either by heaven, for it is God's throne; 35 or by the earth, for it is his footstool; or by Jerusalem, for it is the city of the Great King. 36 And do not swear by your head, for you cannot make even one hair white or black. 37 Simply let your 'Yes' be 'Yes,' and your 'No', 'No'; anything beyond this comes from the evil one (Matthew 5:33–37).

An oath was a heightened form of confirming the truth of one's words, whether one was affirming something about the past or promising to do something in the future. The Old Testament frequently endorses the use of oaths in both legal and private settings (Ex 13:19; 22:11; Lev 5:4; Deut 23:21–23; 1 Sam 20:3). The notion of *heightened* truth telling, however, could obviously be interpreted to mean that some forms of speaking the 'truth' were less serious, less binding. This problem already begins to be addressed by the Old Testament prophets (Jer 5:2; Zech 5:3–4).

By James' day an elaborate system of oath-swearing had developed in which truthfulness could be graded according to the type of oath given. Swearing by Jerusalem or by the temple, for instance, was regarded as a *non*-binding oath. On the other hand, swearing by the gold of the temple or by some of the utensils used in the temple was considered fully binding. Other oaths involved swearing by 'heaven' or by 'earth', as James indicates here (see Matthew 23:16–22 and the texts in the Jewish Mishnah: *Nedarim* 1:3; *Shabuot* 4:13; *Sanhedrin* 3:2).

The result of this system was that low level oaths, such as ones invoking Jerusalem, could be used to avoid telling the truth. It is in this context that Jesus rejected the first century oath-system entirely, claiming in Matthew 5:37 that it had its origins in the 'devil', the father of lies. James reaffirms his brother's teaching knowing full well that many in his audience had been raised with the Jewish rules governing oaths. All that is permitted for believers, says James (following Jesus), is a simple 'yes' or 'no'.

James offers an extrapolation of Jesus' teaching in the final part of the verse. If the graded oath system came from the devil, continued participation in the system will, says James, lead to judgment: 'you will be condemned.' The NIV provides an imprecise translation at this point. Literally, our text says: 'Let your "Yes"' be yes, and your "No", no, *so that you may not fall under judgment.*' Those who participate in the satanic system of oaths (designed as it was to permit half-truths) will fall under the judgment of God. Those who abandon that system and commit afresh to the Messiah's simple ethic of honesty will avoid such condemnation. Of course, telling the truth does not earn our salvation but it does reveal the people destined for salvation: those who have been born through the 'word of truth' (1:18) will in obedience to that word live truthfully. This is the logic of James' ethical outlook.

REFLECTIONS

1. Oaths today. Are all oaths wrong in themselves? While some sects believe they are (notably, the Jehovah's Witnesses), this conclusion is difficult to sustain in the light of (a) the original Old Testament context of oaths (mentioned previously); (b) the New Testament's tacit endorsement of some oaths (Acts 2:30; Heb 6:13–16; 7:20– 22, 28); and (c) the Apostle Paul's own use of a solemn oath in Romans 9:2 ('I speak the truth in Christ—I am not lying, my conscience confirms it in the Holy Spirit ...'). It is certainly true that the oath-system of first century Judaism was forbidden to the early Christians. By implication, any system of graded truthfulness (i.e. where some oaths are deliberately considered more binding than others) must also be shunned by Christians. However, it is unlikely that the teaching of James and Jesus was ever intended to rule out all forms of oath-swearing.

2. Truth today. More important than the question of oath-swearing is the biblical insistence that believers always tell the truth. Their 'yes' must always mean yes and their 'no', no. It hardly needs saying that we live in a culture with a high tolerance for lies. In this context, we would do well to recall the high premium placed on truth-telling by James and Jesus. There is no such thing as graded truthfulness and, despite the growing acceptance of obfuscation and 'little white lies', Christians must commit themselves afresh to the principle of speaking truthfully at all times. If we are not known for speaking words of truth, how can we believably claim to know the Word of truth.

QUESTIONS FOR DISCUSSION

1. It was suggested above that 5:12 is a lone instruction with no significant relation to what comes before or after in the letter. Do you agree? Why/why not?
2. Read Matthew 5:34–37. How are James' words similar to and different from those of Jesus? Are the differences at all significant?

12

The Path of Restoration

James 5:13–20

In the final two sections of the letter James (1) issues some parting instructions about how to respond to the joys and pains of life (5:13–18), before (2) concluding with an encouragement to keep the teaching of this precious biblical book alive in the congregation long after the scroll was rolled up and the page closed (5:19–20).

WHEN SOMEONE IS SUFFERING (5:13A)

James begins his closing remarks with a brief word to the person in distress: 'Is any one of you in trouble? He should pray' (5:13).

The word rendered 'trouble' is actually the word 'suffering'. It is the same word translated 'suffering' in 5:10 just three verses earlier. James, then, is not referring to any momentary inconvenience but to the experience of real hardship or distress, whether poverty, persecution, bereavement, betrayal or the like.

According to James, the godly person responds to trouble with prayer (verse 13). Notice, however, that James says nothing about *what* to pray. There are numerous different terms for 'prayer' in the New Testament—petition, thanksgiving, intercession, confession, praise and others. James here employs the general term (*proseuchomai*), the one covering all forms of address to God. Thus, James is not necessarily exhorting the sufferer to petition God for deliverance—as appropriate as that might be; he is simply urging believers to approach God with their pain in whatever way is appropriate. The Old Testament Book of Psalms—the prayer book of ancient Israel—has almost as many prayerful *laments* as it does straightforward petitions. Both can be expressions of devotion to the Lord, and sometimes the former is the only type of prayer a sufferer feels able to utter.

WHEN SOMEONE IS JOYFUL (5:13B)

The second half of verse 13 addresses another person altogether, and this believer is urged to offer a *specific* form of prayer: 'Is anyone happy? Let him sing songs of praise' (5:13).

Just as the pains of life should turn the believer toward prayer, so should its joys. The Scriptures sometimes warn against spiritual 'forgetfulness' when life is going well (Deut 6:10–12). The antidote to this comfortable amnesia is 'praise', turning our joys into opportunities to give God the glory.

The expression 'sing songs of praise' translates a single Greek verb, *psallō*, the verb form of the word 'psalm'. It means, of course, to declare one's thankfulness to God usually by way of a song appropriate to the occasion. The Book of Psalms contains many such songs but countless others had been composed (by Jews and Christians) by the time James penned these words (possibly including Phil 2:6–11 and Col 1:15–20) and, doubtless, his hearers had a significant repertoire to choose from.

Interestingly, James' exhortation is directed to an individual: 'Let *him* sing songs of praise.' This leaves open the possibility that James means to include songs sung to the Lord in private. The point should not be pushed, however, since 'praise' is more naturally an activity of the gathered people of God. Perhaps what James has in mind is that the joyful individual, out of gratitude to the Lord, suggests a song of praise to be sung by the whole church. A similar scenario is envisaged by Paul in 1 Corinthians 14:26 ('When you come together, *everyone one has a hymn* or word of instruction, a revelation, a tongue or an interpretation. Let all things be done for building up').

WHEN SOMEONE IS ILL (5:14–18)

In verse 14 James turns to encourage another type of prayer—intercession for the sick:

> 14 Is any one of you sick? He should call the elders of the church to pray over him and anoint him with oil in the name of the Lord. 15 And the prayer offered in faith will make the sick person well; the Lord will raise him up (5:14–15).

The word translated 'sick' in verse 14 *can* mean simply 'weak' (2 Cor 11:21; 13:3–9), and the word translated 'make well' in verse 15 can mean simply 'restore'. Because of this some interpreters, perhaps keen to discourage the excesses of some modern healing movements, have proposed that this paragraph be read as a discussion of *spiritual* weakness and *spiritual* restoration.

This interpretation has failed to convince many New Testament commentators. While the 'sick-well' language of James 5 can conceivably mean 'weak-restored', it is not the usual sense of the words. Of particular significance is the fact that James' word 'sick' (*astheneō*) is the default term throughout the Jesus-tradition (from which James draws so much) for an illness healed by the Lord (Matthew 10:8; 25:36, 39; Mark 6:56; Luke 4:40; John 4:46; 5:3–7 and many others). Before assigning *possible* meanings to biblical terms there must be good reasons for excluding their *natural* meanings. In the case of James 5:14 there is none, especially since, as all commentators acknowledge, the practice of healing the sick was a vibrant tradition in early Christianity (Luke 9:6; Acts 3:1–8; 1 Cor 12:9, 28, 30). To avoid placing this passage within that tradition involves special pleading.

In 5:14–15 James is not referring to a special gift or office of healing. He is talking rather about a simple ministry of prayer exercised by 'elders', that is, by the leading members of the Christian community (e.g. Acts 20:17). The sick person, says James, is to 'call' the elders (verse 14). This expression suggests that the person is suffering a grave illness, one which does not allow him to get up and go to the elders himself. The elders come, pray for the person, anoint him or her with oil (cf. Isa 1:6) and this 'will make the sick person well; the Lord will raise him up'. The expression 'raise up' (in connection with healing) may have come to James via the stories of Jesus' healings where the same term frequently appears (Matthew 9:5–7; Mark 3:3; 5:41; John 5:8). The practice of anointing the sick with oil was common enough in first century Judaism and is reflected in Jesus' own instructions to his apostles (Mark 6:13).

The prayer of the elders on behalf of the sick is said to be a prayer 'of faith'. This means more than a psychological 'confidence' that the prayer will be answered. Given James' discussion of what true faith involves (2:14–26), a prayer of faith is a request to God born out of true devotion to him. The reference to 'the prayer of a righteous man' in verse 16 means much the same thing. It is the prayers of the devout, those that walk in God's ways, that James has in mind here.

James adds a further benefit of the prayer for healing: 'If he (the sick person) has sinned, he will be forgiven' (verse 15). How are sin and healing connected in this passage? While many ancient cultures frequently connected sickness with wrongdoing, the Bible does not share this mechanistic, karmic view of reality. Indeed, the Old Testament Book of Job roundly rejects the common sin-sickness equation. Nevertheless, from a very different set of assumptions the Scriptures do teach that illness *can* on occasion be related to disobedience. For instance, when the wealthy Christians of Corinth turned the Lord's Supper into a drunken banquet from which the poor were excluded, the Apostle Paul warns:

> 29 anyone who eats and drinks without recognising the body of the Lord eats and drinks judgment on himself. 30 That is why many among you are weak and sick ... (1 Cor 11:29–30).

James appears to reflect this perspective. Flagrant disobedience of God, such as that in Corinth and amongst some in James' audience, *may* result in sickness. This will not be a karmic reaping of what one sows but God's fatherly discipline intended to humble the wayward believer. The 'if' of verse 15, then, is important. James is not saying that some people sin and others do not. He is rather saying that *if* the illness in question is a result of the sufferer's sin, the request for healing will function as an act of repentance and so will bring forgiveness. Quite unlike the pagan culture surrounding him, James does not *assume* that the sickness comes from sin; he simply regards it as a possibility, one which can be resolved through confession and prayer.

As a health measure, therefore, James immediately adds a call to collective confession, prayer and healing:

> Therefore confess your sins to each other and pray for each other so that you may be healed. The prayer of a righteous man is powerful and effective (5:16).

It is interesting that, having emphasised the ministry of elders in verse 14, James now speaks more generally of the role of the wider congregation toward 'each other'. Hearing confessions and praying for forgiveness (and healing) are functions belonging to the whole church. James apparently envisages his readers being open with one another (as well as with God: 4:7–10) about the extent to which they have been party to the sins denounced throughout the letter. Most of the evils mentioned in the epistle are 'community' sins; the remedy therefore is community confession and prayer (resulting in healing where appropriate).

James emphasises in verse 16 that it is the prayer of the 'righteous' person that is powerful and effective (for healing). Frequently in the New Testament the term 'righteous' is an exclusively *theological* tag, describing those who are *in the right* with God purely on account of God's covenant grace (e.g. Rom 1:17; 5:19). Just as frequently, however, the Bible employs what you might call a *descriptive* usage of the term 'righteous'. Here, the word describes someone who devotedly (but not unfailingly) walks in the paths of God (Matthew 1:19; Luke 1:6; 2:25; 23:50; Acts 10:22; Titus 1:8; 1 Pet 3:12; 4:18; 1 John 3:7, 12). There is no suggestion here that the 'righteous' person is free from sin;

the term simply describes the believer's commitment to God's ways. This, of course, includes repentance when one sins. This descriptive usage of 'righteous' is not separate from the theological usage. Within biblical logic, the person who has been declared right with God (through Christ) will (through the Spirit) walk in the ways of God. The point is: in James 5:16 the prayer which is 'powerful and effective', the one which is willingly heard by the Lord, is that offered by a person devoted to the paths of God. In this way, the prayer of the 'righteous' is virtually synonymous with the prayer 'offered in faith' (verse 15).

In verses 17–18 James provides an Old Testament example of his point:

> 17 Elijah was a man just like us. He prayed earnestly that it would not rain, and it did not rain on the land for three and a half years. 18 Again he prayed, and the heavens gave rain, and the earth produced its crops (5:17–18).

James recalls a story from Elijah's life well known to his audience (1 Kings 17–18) and offers it as proof that a normal human being (as distinct from, say, an angelic being) can be involved in abnormal events in God's world. Ordinary people devoted to the path of the Almighty can witness extraordinary things when they pray. The reference to the breaking of a drought and the production of crops is apt for a discussion of healing, for it reminds us of God's ability to renew his creation, whether the dry earth or the frail human body.

Verses 17–18, then, serve as an encouragement to approach God for healing. James must have known that not *all* of the prayers of the righteous are answered in the way hoped for (cf. 2 Cor 12:7–9), but he makes his point in absolute terms ('the Lord *will* raise him up'), because he wants to inspire action and confidence in prayer.

WHEN SOMEONE WANDERS (5:19–20)

Having spoken of the one who is suffering, the one who is happy and the one who is ill, James concludes the letter with a brief paragraph about the one who has departed from true faith. And here James provides a key to ensuring that the teaching of this letter lives on long after we close the book:

> 19 My brothers, if one of you should wander from the truth and someone should bring him back, 20 remember this: Whoever turns a sinner from the error of his way will save him from death and cover over a multitude of sins. (5:19–20)

These words may seem an odd way to end the letter, especially when compared with the warm and personal 'goodbyes' found in the letters of Paul (e.g. Rom 16:3–24; 1 Cor 16:21–24; 2 Cor 13:11–14; 1 Thess 5:25–28). We must remember, however, that the epistle of James was not a personal correspondence to dear friends, as most of Paul's letters were. It was an authoritative circular from the brother of Jesus and pillar of early Christianity to believers throughout the Jewish Diaspora, some of whom were engaging in the most hypocritical acts imaginable. They had been showing favouritism to the rich and publicly shaming the poor (2:1–13). Worse: they had been ignoring the plight of the poor (2:14–26) as they fought against each other with poisonous tongues (3:1–12) in an effort to amass wealth and increase pleasure (4:1–3). In short, the Christians to whom James wrote were defying the defining principle of the Christian life: the royal law of love (2:8). In this context, the final paragraph is the perfect conclusion. What James himself has been doing throughout the letter he urges his readers now to do for one another: seek out wayward brothers and sisters and turn them back to 'the truth'.

The 'truth' referred to in verse 19 is not a doctrinal truth. Nothing in the letter suggests James' audience was in danger of heresy. The 'truth' here must be reference to the 'word of truth' (1:18) and the 'perfect law that gives freedom' (1:25); it is the truth of the Jesus-tradition itself, by which James' readers had received new birth and from which this epistle has drawn so much of its style, content and force. The 'wandering' mentioned in this verse, then, is primarily ethical. It refers to departing from the lifestyle demanded of the follower of Jesus.

The letter of James has been calling on believers to conform to the truth of Jesus. The final paragraph urges readers to take up that purpose themselves and seek to win back to the right path those who have strayed—who perhaps are no longer even present in the congregation and so were unable to hear James' message as it was read out.

The wayward person is called a 'sinner'. When used of a believer (as here and in 4:8) this term implies a gross refusal to submit to God's ways, as previously noted. It does not refer to the typical Christian who devotedly, albeit imperfectly, follows God's path. It describes the brother or sister who defies the teaching of Jesus without repentance. It is the person who claims to have faith 'without deeds'. James has already said that the faith of such a person is dead (2:17). Now he warns that the fate of such a one may indeed be 'death' (5:20), that is, exclusion from the kingdom of God.

James therefore calls on faithful Christians to 'save' their sinful counterparts from this terrible fate by 'turning' them from the 'error' of their ways. In other words, believers are to do what they can, presumably by word and example as well as by prayer, to influence wayward brothers and sisters back to the path of Christ. Doing so will 'cover over' the multitude of their sins. To have sins 'covered' is a biblical expression for divine forgiveness (Ps 32:1; 85:2; Rom 4:7). It refers to God's willingness to conceal in his presence the faults of the repentant sinner. Again in James' letter, the offer of mercy is never far away from the threat of judgment.

REFLECTIONS

1. Prayer in trouble. Some religious traditions, notably Buddhism, insist that one's experience of pain is overcome by negating our desire for the things of this world. Live with detachment towards the self and towards the world, taught the Buddha, and suffering will evaporate. There are of course secular strategies for dulling the pain. This usually involves the pursuit of momentary pleasures or increased wealth. Christians, however, avoid both extremes. We neither detach from God's world, nor crave its fleeting pleasures. Instead, we pray, as James 5:13 instructs. We bring the reality of our troubles directly and honestly to our heavenly Father and seek his comfort and resolution. Believers who avoid approaching God with their pain are only shortchanging themselves.

2. Songs of praise. The New Testament portrays psalm-singing as a normative and important practice of Jesus (Matthew 26:30), the apostles (Acts 16:25) and, especially, the early Christian congregations (Rom 15:5–11; 1 Cor 14:15, 26; Eph 5:19–20; Col 3:16). James' exhortation to 'sing songs of praise' (5:13) fits neatly within this picture. Singing 'psalms, hymns and spiritual songs' (Col 3:16) is an essential part of the Christian gathering. It is an expression of thankfulness, according to James 5:13, Eph 5:20 and Col 3:16, as well as being a mode of corporate instruction. This latter point is especially clear in Colossians 3:16 wherein the call to 'sing psalms, hymns, and spiritual songs' is dependent (grammatically as well as logically) on the introductory exhortation: 'Let the word of Christ dwell in you richly.' Songs of praise are not mere 'fillers' for the hour long church service; they are a core expression of the vertical and horisontal purposes of our gathering.

3. Healing in the church. The obvious question arising from James 5:14–15 is: should the modern church institute regular ministries of healing as outlined in these verses? The answer is: yes and no. You will notice that James does not address his words to the elders of the church,

as if there were some official institution and liturgy of healing which they were obliged to perform on a regular basis. The exhortation is addressed to the congregation itself and to the sick person in particular. 'When one of you falls ill,' says James, 'you call for the elders'. Hence, prayer (with anointing) for healing is a ministry exercised at the request of the church member. The issue is not whether ministers set up a healing programme but whether we as the members of the church ask for the service described in these verses. Having said that, notice also that James exhorts the entire congregation in verse 16: 'confess your sins to each other and pray for each other so that you may be healed.' Elders may have a little more time on their hands to be involved in this ministry but all of us should be willing to be involved.

4. *Mutual accountability.* What James asks of his readers in the final paragraph (5:19–20) goes completely against our modern, individualistic culture. We talk about faith as a 'private affair'. We say, 'Who am I to judge?' We even quote Jesus, 'Take the plank out of your own eye', forgetting that he then added, 'then you will see clearly to remove the speck from your brother's eye' (Matthew 7:3–5). Naturally, we should never be judgmental and hypocritical toward others, but the Christian community should be a place of mutual accountability. We are meant to be a family and part of being a family is helping each other stay on track, not only through prayer and example, the principal means of godly influence, but also through humble confrontation and criticism, 'turning sinners' from their error, as James says.

EPILOGUE

The word of truth found in the Jesus tradition, and restated in the epistle of James, has claims over the whole of life. After a tantalising foretaste of the themes of the letter (1:1–27), James has pleaded with believers not to favour the rich as the world so often does (2:1–13) but to demonstrate true faith by works of compassion towards the poor (2:14–26). The same compassion must govern the tongue also, says James (3:1–12): would-be teachers are to think twice about assuming such a role and believers are to speak to their neighbours as fellow bearers of the divine likeness. Moreover, they are to work for peace in all their relationships, practising what James calls deeds done in the humility that comes from true wisdom (3:13–18).

This wisdom, rightly grasped, will put an end to the harmful pursuit of wealth and pleasure (4:1–3), demanding of us an unqualified submission to the God who opposes the proud and lifts up the humble (4:4–10), leaving us without a basis for human slander and judgment (4:11–12). The upwardly mobile will keep their aspirations in check (4:13–17), while the faithful oppressed will wait patiently for the overthrow of tyranny at the coming of the Lord (5:1–12). The troubled will pray, the joyful will sing and the sick will find healing and forgiveness in the prayers of the church (5:13–18).

But the impact of James does not end with the close of his book; it continues on through those who have grasped its message. That's what 5:19–20 is about. By ending the letter the way he does—urging the faithful to win back the wayward—James lifts himself out of the picture and hands the work of the epistle over to his hearers: now we must seek to restore family members back to the Messiah's royal law of love. The real work of the Book of James, therefore, begins now.

QUESTIONS FOR DISCUSSION

1. With James 5:13 and Colossians 3:17 in mind, what place should singing have in our Christian lives?
2. Keeping in mind James' understanding of faith, what is the connection between prayer and faith in 5:15?
3. What is the connection between sin and sickness in 5:15?
4. What is the purpose of 5:19–20 in the epistle as a whole?
5. How do you suppose James envisages believers 'bringing back' those who have wandered from the truth?

Notes

Notes

Notes

Notes

Notes

Notes